BRITAIN YESTERDAY&TODAY

THIS IS A CARLTON BOOK

Design copyright © 2003, 2005 Carlton Books Ltd
Text copyright © 2003, 2005 Janice Anderson &
Edmund Swinglehurst

This edition published in 2006 for Index Books Ltd
by Carlton Books Ltd
20 Mortimer Street
London
W1T 3JW

First published in 2003

A CIP catalogue for this book is available from the
British Library.

ISBN10: 1 84442 106 6
ISBN13: 978 1 84442 106 0

Art Editor: Vicky Holmes
Project Editor: Amie McKee
Design: Brian Flynn
Editorial: Rob Dimery
Picture research: Adrian Bentley
Production: Lucy Woodhead

Printed in Singapore

BRITAIN YESTERDAY & TODAY

JANICE ANDERSON &
EDMUND SWINGLEHURST

CARLTON
BOOKS

CONTENTS

FREE TIME **1**

1890
Donkey rides on the sands were a popular feature of days by the sea. These donkeys are on the main beach at Blackpool.

GREAT DAYS OUT

Before the railway age, days off were spent locally for most Britons, if they took them at all. The train enabled people to get away quickly to the countryside and the seaside. The 1871 Bank Holidays Act, which established the Easter, Whitsun, August and Christmas bank holidays, gave another fillip to the idea of taking a short break from home and work.

The seaside was the most popular destination for days out in Britain and all the big resorts catered as much for the day visitor as for the longer-term holidaymaker. Margate and Southend, downriver from London, Brighton on the south coast and Blackpool in the north were among the most popular resorts.

While a trip to the seaside is still a great day out, more sophisticated day trippers have their search for excitement met by all the fun of the theme park. The great theme parks, such as Alton Towers in Staffordshire and Thorpe Park in Surrey, offer a dazzling array of rides, entertainments and other attractions that quieter suppliers of great days out, such as the National Trust, cannot match.

TODAY
Theme parks provide today's great days out. Intrepid visitors are turned upside down when they ride on the 'Air' rollercoaster at Alton Towers.

HOLIDAY CAMPS

Billy Butlin launched the first of his many holiday camps at Skegness in 1936 and one at Clacton-on-Sea two years later. His camps and those people who followed him, such as the holiday giant Thomas Cook, provided clean, simple holiday accommodation in wood cabins at a time when life was hard for many.

After the war was over in 1945, holiday camps were hugely popular, offering all kinds of entertainments and fun for all ages, from knobbly knees competitions and bathing beauty pageants to ballroom dancing and light entertainments, day and night.

The advent of the cheap package holiday abroad in the 1960s meant the end of the old-style Butlins camp. People wanted freedom, not the constant attention of regiments of blazered hosts making everyone 'join in'.

Today's holiday camp is a very different being. It is called a 'holiday leisure resort' and it is built with the British weather in mind. At a Center Parc, for instance, visitors can indulge in water sports and games in a sub-tropical climate, oblivious of any snow or rain outside.

15

1953
Bankside Power Station ten years from completion. It was powered by oil rather than coal, a controversial system in the 1950s.

TATE MODERN

The transformation of Bankside Power Station on the south bank of the Thames into Tate Modern began in 1995. The art gallery was opened in the Millennium year, 2000, but the footbridge that was meant to link it to the north bank near St Paul's Cathedral had to be closed because it swung too much. It opened to the public in 2002, since when it has been a hugely popular way of reaching the gallery.

The Bankside Power Station, designed by architect Sir Giles Gilbert Scott, was built in two phases between 1947 and 1963. It is a brick-clad steel structure, with some 4.2 million bricks used in its construction. The main chimney was kept down to a height of 325 feet (99 metres) so that it would be lower than Sir Christopher Wren's dome on St Paul's.

The building was transformed into a truly exciting gallery of modern art by world-famous Swiss architects Herzog & de Meuron. Their greatest change was to add a two-storey glass structure spanning the length of the roof, which lets natural light into the galleries and houses a café offering spectacular views across London.

TODAY
Tate Modern at night, seen from the St Paul's Cathedral end of the Millennium Bridge. The gallery is open late on Fridays and Saturdays.

This elegant party picnicking at
Stonehenge includes Queen Victoria's
son, Prince Leopold, Duke of Albany
(reclining on his elbow, cigar in hand).

MYSTERIOUS STONEHENGE

The great circle of stones called Stonehenge
that stands in a field on the Salisbury Plain in
Wiltshire is one of the most important
survivals from pre-historic times in Britain. It
has long attracted thousands of visitors every
year, not least those seeking some remnant of
the sun-worshipping Druids.

Druids held sun-worshipping ceremonies at
Stonehenge nearly four thousand years ago.
Today, Companions of the Most Ancient Order
of Druids keep vigil at Stonehenge every
June 21, the day of the summer solstice.

The wear and tear caused by the huge
numbers of tourists who visit the site every
year has led to the creation of some very
controversial schemes for visitor management
in recent years, including an underground
tunnel leading from a car park and the
obligatory visitors' centre some distance
from the site.

TODAY

Police were present in strength in
2001 at a revival of the ancient
Druids' way of celebrating the
summer solstice at Stonehenge.

MUSIC ON THE BEACH

Before the invention of batteries, transistor
radios and printed circuits, the way to get your
own dance music on to the beach was to take
out your wind-up gramophone, a selection of
records – which in the days before vinyl were
heavy and easily broken – and a box of needles.

Of course, the sound would not travel very
far and could be blown away on the wind, but
you would have the advantage of dancing to
the latest dance band music, rather than to the
less fashionable sounds that might be coming
from the seaside bandstand.

Modern sound systems can send music at
full volume across acres of crowded beach,
and summertime rock and pop concerts and
other happenings have become very popular,
attracting hundreds of thousands of young
people. A massive beach music party in
Brighton in 2002 attracted 250,000 people
to the town and brought it to a standstill.
Life's a beach, indeed.

ASTORIA

AL JOLSON & DAVEY LEE
THE SINGING FOOL
COMMENCING AUGUST 19TH

VARIETY

CINEMA

THE SINGING FOOL & DETECTIVES SUNDAYS 5.30

ASTORIA

ASTORIA

Fans queue round the block at the
Astoria in Brixton, south London, to
see variety entertainer Al Jolson's
second 'talkie', *The Singing Fool.*

THE CINEMA

Moving pictures were first shown in Britain in
darkened halls, variety theatres, fairgrounds
and 'penny gaffs'. The first cinemas – with
padded seats, fluted columns and potted ferns,
and with a pianist or even a musical trio in
attendance – gave way in the twenties to a
wonderful riot of styles, from Spanish and
Mexican to Art Deco and 'Odeon' modernist.

Cinema-going in Britain today, with ticket
sales soaring, is a very different experience.
The cinema is more likely to be a vast, multi-
screen complex on the edge of town than a
theatre-like building on the high street. Movie-
goers, with their tickets bought via phone or
the Internet, park within yards of the entrance,
arm themselves with buckets of popcorn and
other delights, and settle themselves in seats
like armchairs, ready to have their senses
assaulted by the effects, on the screen and in
the cinema, of the latest advances in
computer-generated film technology. The
cinema is once again as exciting (though perhaps
less glamorous) as it was in the thirties, when it
first became part of the national culture.

TODAY

The splendid Warners cinema in
London's Leicester Square was
converted into a multi-screen to
meet modern cinema demands.

1932

Two sisters send their hoops bowling along a path popular with children and their mothers and nannies in Hyde Park, London.

PLAYING IN THE PARK

Providing fresh air and fun for children became an objective of early Victorian town planners, horrified by the appalling conditions in which so many people in Britain's towns lived.

Increasing numbers of parks and gardens, hitherto usually privately owned, were opened for everyone to enjoy. Manchester, for instance, opened three public parks in 1846, all paid for by public subscription. One of them, Peel Park, included among the trees and flowerbeds swings and see-saws for children and areas set aside for ninepins, bowls and gymnastics.

Play areas in parks still have a big part to play in children's well-being. The fight today is against the results of affluence. Too much fast food, too much sitting in front of TV and computer screens and too little exercise is making children fat. The brightly painted, cleverly designed play areas are there to attract children away from their television and computer screens and out into the park.

TODAY

Children have fun in a colourful, well-designed play area in the Moors Valley Country Park, near Ringwood in Hampshire.

LOWRY'S WORLD

Although a city in its own right, with a charter granted in 1230 and an important part played in the creation of Britain's industrial wealth, Salford has become almost submerged in the urban sprawl of Greater Manchester.

This once-grimy centre of industry became a big star in the arts firmament when the Lowry arts complex was opened at Salford Quays. L S Lowry, who was born in Salford in 1887, began his working life as a clerk but soon turned to art, training in Manchester. In hundreds of drawings and paintings he recorded the life of the Lancashire industrial scene. Many of his paintings are peopled with ant-like crowds of stick figures scurrying among factories and grimy buildings. He was made a Royal Academician in 1962 in recognition of his unique contribution to art.

The Lowry was built in 1999 with the help of a £64 million grant from National Lottery funding. Set in the heart of the re-developed Salford Quays, the Lowry is a centre for performing and visual arts and the place to go to see some of L S Lowry's finest work in the world that inspired it.

IN THE GARDEN

'Our England is a garden ... full of borders, beds and shrubberies,' wrote Rudyard Kipling. His countrymen tried to emulate nature rather than formalize it, in the Continental style, in their home gardens. Herbaceous borders were planted with tall hollyhocks, lupins and delphiniums, while petunias, carnations and pansies spilled over on to paths. Pergolas draped with honeysuckle, rambler roses and clematis provided gardens with private areas where ladies, wearing bonnets to protect their faces from the sun, could enjoy moments of quiet.

Until the mid-twentieth century, gardeners were widely employed, but rising wages and alternative job opportunities caused their disappearance. Today, everyone is their own gardener. Inspired by TV gardeners, at weekends they head for garden centres, which have blossomed under the influence of television, radio and newspaper gardening experts.

The Chelsea Flower Show has been a top gardening (and social) event since its inception in 1913. Today's show runs for five days, and on the last day everything is sold off to the garden-loving public.

TODAY
A futuristic water garden at a recent Chelsea Flower Show, where landscape gardening and cutting-edge furniture design are also on show.

1937

Escaping an August heatwave, this angler, still in his working suit, lets one of his three rods look after itself while he dozes among the bulrushes.

ANGLING

The soothing experience of a day's fishing has been enjoyed by country folk and townspeople alike for centuries. Enthusiasm for the pastime grew in the nineteenth century and steps toward its regulation began. For the better-off, land-owning classes, fishing meant fishing for salmon and trout on private stretches of rivers. The ordinary fish of rivers and streams, such as perch, carp and pike, provided coarse fishing for everyone else.

Village shops near rivers began to carry stocks of rods, reels, lines and floats. Specialist shops were opened and the first angling magazines were published, giving advice on how and where to fish.

Today, a licence is always needed for anyone fishing for salmon and trout. Coarse fishing on streams and rivers usually requires a water-authority licence, too, but the fee is modest and easily obtained. Many anglers opt for fishing specially stocked, privately run lakes and reservoirs. Wherever the setting, outwitting the wily denizens of inland waters is always a challenge for the fishermen's patience.

TODAY

The green umbrellas sheltering these Thames anglers are a familiar sight along riverbanks and around lakes and reservoirs in Britain.

1918
Bathers enjoying the simple
pleasures of life, playing ring-a-roses
at the shallow end of the lido at
Southport, in Lancashire.

SWIMMING

The idea that swimming could be good for the
nation's health was given a boost in the early
nineteenth century by the fashion for sea-
bathing, the health values of which were
extolled in several best-selling books. The six
public baths opened in London in 1837 were a
sign that local authorities had taken their
words to heart.

Public baths were built for practical rather
than fashionable reasons and many of them
provided lessons in swimming and life-saving.
The sexes were kept separate and women
wore bloomers and black stockings in the
pool. By 1910, a one-piece woollen swimming
costume was universally accepted as
respectable wear for men and women.

Open-air pools with lidos, many of them in
Art Deco style, gave a touch of Continental
sophistication to public baths between the
wars. But this was nothing compared to the
excitements of today's leisure centre
swimming pools. Wave machines, giant slides,
flumes and much else has turned swimming
into a fun day out as well as healthy exercise.

TODAY
The Kingfisher Leisure Pool at
Sudbury in Suffolk has the flume,
wave machine and inflatable raft
that bathers expect of pools today.

Couples dine and dance the night away in style at the elegant Palm Beach Café, on the bank of the Thames in London.

DANCING THE HOURS AWAY

Dancing was hugely popular in between-the-wars Britain. Enjoyed by the well-off in the privacy of nightclubs, hotels and the local tennis or sailing club, it was taken up with enthusiasm by ordinary folk in vast 'palais de dance'. In fact, the dance hall, where young people could go 'courting', was almost as popular as the cinema, where the back row often meant 'two penn'orth of darkness'.

At grander functions, a full orchestra, often with a leader made famous by radio, supplied the music, which was as likely to be the new quickstep, foxtrot and tango as the waltz.

There is not much dancing in the vast caverns that are today's clubs, nor is there a big orchestra in a scene where the DJ, with a stack of discs and a great line in patter, is king. The excitement comes from the assault on the senses of music played at high-decibel volume, and of the flickering of multi-coloured strobe lighting and laser beams in a dark and crowded place so hot that the experienced clubber wears clothes with air vents in them.

TODAY

The DJ rather than the band is king in the modern club. Formal dancing is a thing of the past – today, everyone does their own thing.

c.1939

No helmets or special leather gear are needed for the riders of these motorbikes, made by AJS, a major manufacturer in the thirties.

MOTORCYCLING

Two developments in the 1920s, the pillion seat and the sidecar, brought the motorcycle within range of the family holidaymaker. A young father not earning enough to be able to afford even a small car could fit his wife and two small children in the sidecar of a motorcycle and place his eldest child safely astride the pillion seat.

As Britain led the world in the manufacture of motorcycles at the time, motorcyclists had a splendid range of makes from which to choose, including AJS, BSA, Matchless, Norton and Triumph.

In the post-war world, the British motorcycle and sidecar lost its place as a useful family runabout. Apart from the increasing competition from foreign motorbike manufacturers, there were many more cheap cars available. The Mini, first produced in 1959, dealt the final blow to the motorcycle-sidecar combination. Today's leather-clad biker would not swap his powerful, ton-up-easy Harley Davidson for anything as unsophisticated and uncool as a motorbike and sidecar.

TODAY

Santa's little helpers in leather, these Harley Davidson riders have just brought Father Christmas to Selfridges in London in roaring style.

1935
A low-flying Hawker Hart biplane gives the crowd a hair-parting thrill at an airshow at the Hendon airfield in north London.

FUN IN THE AIR

Taking to the air in a flying machine caught the public imagination in the 1920s. Many pilots from the Royal Flying Corps (re-named the Royal Air Force in 1918) found new work at airshows, demonstrating the capabilities of the biplanes that had taken part in World War I, and even offering aerial flips for a few shillings.

Much of this kind of flying was done from farm fields, or from the long, flat beaches of resorts such as Tenby in Wales. Flying displays were regular events at two former military airfields in London, Hendon and Northolt.

As flying became more commonplace, simply going up into the air for a few minutes lost its attraction. From 1948, the public's greater expectations were met for fifty years by the annual Farnborough Air Show, with its flying displays at the frontiers of technology. At the same time, fine air museums such as the Royal Air Force Museum at Hendon and the Imperial War Museum's air museum at Duxford in Cambridgeshire, were taking shape. Today, their displays, in the air and on the ground, recreate the thrill of flying for everyone.

TODAY
The Royal Air Force's acrobatic flying team, the Red Arrows, provides a patriotic flash of red, white and blue during a display.

39

1892
The Temperate House at Kew
Gardens was opened in 1860. By
1892, the House's Central Walk
was dwarfed by its plants.

GREAT BOTANIC GARDENS

The world's first horticultural garden began as a private botanic garden laid out along the Thames in the grounds of Kew Palace by Augusta, Princess of Wales.

Today, the Royal Botanic Gardens at Kew is a major horticultural and botanic institution and a fine public garden. Among Kew's many attractions are several glasshouses, ranging from Decimus Burton's great Palm House of 1848 to the Princess of Wales Conservatory, named after Princess Augusta and opened by Diana, Princess of Wales in 1987.

Since 2000, Kew's glasshouses have been rivalled for garden lovers' attention by the giant domes, called biomes, of the Eden Project in Cornwall. Essentially a conservatory of the world's ecological systems, the Eden Project attracts some two million visitors a year to its two biomes, devoted to the humid tropics and the warm temperate zone. A third biome is planned, for the dry tropics.

TODAY
Dawn breaks above the humid
tropics biome at the Eden Project,
built in a disused china clay pit near
St Austell in Cornwall.

41

A crisp white shirt and tie and a stylish straw boater was the standard dress worn by Victorian ladies when cycling in the countryside.

CYCLING

The invention of the safety bicycle with a protected chain guard in the 1870s brought the age of universal cycling into being. Even Prime Minister Gladstone approved, saying that cycling offered almost unbounded benefits, physically, morally and socially.

Mr Gladstone had only men in mind, but soon women were as enthusiastic cyclists as men, the 'New Women' among them going as far as adopting the American Mrs Amelia Bloomer's splendid trousers for cycling wear. For the Victorian man, the cycling club became a major attraction of the weekends. Men liked the competitive aspect of the cycling club, which included cycling round specially built oval circuits and taking part in long-distance cross-country rallies.

The present-day popularity of leisure-time cycling, spurred on by the invention of the mountain bike, has led to the building of a National Cycle Network, which will eventually cover the whole country; the first five thousand miles of the network were officially opened in 2000.

TODAY

Two helmeted cyclists on mountain bikes splash through a ford on a forest track near Ballachulish in the Scottish Highlands.

RADIO & SOUND

Before the music record and the radio, the family home was a quiet place. The gramophone, originally a cylinder with a stylus that could record sound then play it back, and then a flat disc played on a turntable, was the first revolution in home entertainment to change all that. It was followed in 1922 by the first radio broadcasts, received by way of large wooden radio sets enclosing glowing valves and and a speaker hidden behind fabric protected by wooden fretwork.

Within four years of those first radio broadcasts, over two million broadcasting receiving licences had been sold in Britain and the BBC Radio Dance Band had been formed. Meanwhile, people who did not have a radio could listen and dance to music played on 78rpm records on their gramophones.

The miniaturization of radios and record players would astonish the pioneers of home music. Today, whole worlds of sound can be stuffed into the corner of a satchel and taken out of the home to be listened to anywhere and at any time their owners want.

TODAY
Schoolchildren take the opportunity of a break in lessons to listen to each other's latest pop and rock music minidiscs and CDs.

45

1890
The column-shaped rocks that form the floor of the Giant's Causeway are so smooth that it is possible to walk across them.

THE GIANT'S CAUSEWAY

The Giant's Causeway lies near the top of any list of must-see sites in the UK. Set on the northern coast of County Antrim, it is where myth and science meet in a mysterious cliffscape of 37,000 hexagonal basalt columns reaching out into the sea.

The island of Staffa, off Scotland's west coast, has a similar columnar rock formation, lending substance to the old myth that a causeway once linked these two ancient kingdoms and was used by the heroic giant Finn MacCool to walk to Scotland in pursuit of his true love and bring her back with him to Ulster.

The truth of the Causeway's formation lies in science. The plateau that makes up much of County Antrim and the northern edge of Ireland was created by an enormous volcanic eruption nearly 60 million years ago. At the Causeway site, the volcanic stone cooled and shrank rapidly, breaking the rock into the even blocks seen by half a million visitors each year.

TODAY
Tourists at the Giant's Causeway, brought to the site by bus from a nearby visitors' centre, a must-have amenity for all leading tourist sites.

1935
The Women's League of Health and Beauty parades 15,000 of its members for a display of physical exercises in London's Hyde Park.

EXERCISE & THE PERFECT SHAPE

Keeping fit and retaining the figures of their youth became a priority for many women from early in the twentieth century. The keep-fit message found its earliest followers in an increasingly militaristic Germany in the 1920s. In England, it was taken up by Mrs Prunella Stack, who organized a women's keep-fit movement to which she gave the deliberately unmilitaristic title of The Women's League of Health and Beauty.

Before long, she had gathered many thousands of women to her cause, happy to take part in mass public demonstrations of physical exercises.

Though such public demonstrations quite quickly lost their appeal, physical fitness allied to a firm body has not, with both men and women filling the exercise rooms of gyms, community leisure centres and private health clubs. Today, more women take part in keep-fit and yoga classes than in any other kind of active sport except walking.

TODAY
Women exercise on running machines in a well-equipped, luxuriously turned-out private health club.

CAMPING

Wheeled transport, first the bicycle then the motor car, helped turn camping into a recreation everyone could enjoy. Long-distance road cycling – a feature of the early days of cycling as a sport – created a need for cyclists' camps, and by 1901 an Association of Cycle Campers had been formed.

The Camping Club of Great Britain and Ireland, still a force in the world of camping today, was established in 1907. A year later the formation of the Boy Scouts movement gave generations of boys the opportunity to learn the skills required for living in tents.

Going camping can mean the whole family enjoying a fortnight's holiday in a multi-roomed tent on a site set up in an area of outstanding natural beauty and equipped with all mod cons, including shops and laundry rooms. It can also mean hikers unstrapping miraculously lightweight tents from their backpacks, unrolling them and setting them up in a remote spot far from any mod cons. Both kinds of camper experience the pleasure of getting away from daily life for a while.

ESSENTIALLY BRITISH **2**

AT THE SEASIDE

By the end of the Edwardian age, mixed bathing had become acceptable at Britain's seaside resorts. Only the most modest woman felt the need to step into the sea from the steps of a bathing machine that had been dragged into the briny by a horse.

The bathing machines, which had been a feature of every English seaside resort since the mid-eighteenth century, were damp, dark and smelly and were not much missed. Many of them had their huge wheels removed and were converted into huts – the provision of shelter being particularly welcome given the unpredictable English summer weather.

Modern beach huts are a much-loved amenity and many of them, being privately owned, fetch large sums when sold. More than just somewhere to change out of wet bathing costumes and store the beach equipment, the modern beach hut may have all the amenities of a summer house, often well furnished and with electricity for lighting and making a cup of tea. The British seaside resorts may have stiff competition from Continental beaches, but they remain very popular.

TODAY
Brightly painted beach huts, some of which may be old bathing machines, are among the amenities of Southwold beach, in Suffolk.

It is June 21, and the parish of
St Botolph, in Bishopsgate, London,
celebrates the summer solstice by
dancing round a maypole.

DANCING ROUND THE MAYPOLE

Pagans danced round trees as part of a tree-worshipping ritual. In Christian times, the worship of nature turned into a celebration of its life-giving force on May Day and at the summer solstice in June. The tree was replaced by a be-ribboned pole for young people to dance round.

Dancing round maypoles – like that other medieval custom, morris dancing – is still very popular in smaller towns and villages. It is a regular feature of primary school fetes, the children putting many hours of practice into getting their dancing right, so that their ribbons wrap themselves in a colourful pattern round the pole.

Since it became an official UK bank holiday, May Day itself is often celebrated in a style more akin to medieval revelry than decorous primary school dancing. May Day again sees young people letting their hair down and dancing in the streets.

TODAY

May Day 2002. These anti-capitalist
demonstrators have opted to use
the bank holiday to march – and
dance – in protest through London.

FISH & CHIPS

The railways relieved Britain's long-standing
problem of how to supply cheap food to
urban workers by quickly moving plentiful
supplies of fish from fishing harbours to the
towns. Fish and chips, bought for a few pence,
sprinkled with vinegar and wrapped in cornets
made from the daily newspaper, became the
favourite meal of the urban working classes.

The supremacy of the fish supper was not
challenged until quite late in the twentieth
century. Cheap package holidays introduced
millions of Britons to different kinds of food
at a time when Indian and Chinese food, the
hamburger and the hot dog were all beginning
to cast their spells over British high streets.

Then the cod, haddock, whiting and plaice
that were the essentials of the fish and chip
business became scarce and expensive. Fish
and chips lost its place as Britain's top dish. It
is still a very popular meal, however, as fish
and chip impresario Harry Ramsden has
successfully demonstrated. His restaurants do
great business from Blackpool to Brighton,
from Heathrow to Hong Kong.

1926

A left-hander, the Duke of York –
later George VI – took part in the
doubles in the 1926 Championships,
partnered by Commander Greig.

WIMBLEDON

The first Wimbledon tennis championships, an
all-Englishmen affair, were held in 1877, on the
grounds of the All-England Croquet Club.
Players from overseas, first from the United
States, then from Australia and New Zealand,
began taking part from the late 1880s.

Although tennis players began changing from
amateurs to professionals in the 1920s in
America, it was not until 1968 that
Wimbledon, one of the world's four 'grand
slam' tournaments, was opened to amateur
and professional players alike. This move,
helped by the arrival of colour television
bounced off satellites to every country in the
world, turned tennis into today's multi-million-
dollar business in which the stars of the game
can quickly become wealthy celebrities.

Wimbledon is the only grand slam tennis
tournament played on grass. So crowded is
the sport's calendar today, that Wimbledon in
2003 was moved back a week to allow more
time for players to adjust from playing on the
French championship's clay to tackling the
former Victorian croquet club's lawn.

TODAY

UK tennis fans provide their heroes
with rousing support. The rise of
talented individuals in recent years
has kept British hopes high.

1926
Nippies serve two of the 1,000
disabled soldiers entertained to tea at
the Coventry Street, London, Lyons
Corner House on December 2.

TEATIME

Tea became a national drink, rather than
something locked away in caddies and teapoys
for a special occasion, when the great, ocean-
going tea clippers began bringing it in bulk
from the Empire's possessions in the East.

Teahouses and tearooms flourished in the
period between the two world wars and Joe
Lyons, who opened his first teashop in
London's Piccadilly, oversaw the building of a
nationwide network of about 250 Lyons
Corner Houses. In the grandest Corner
Houses, staffed by waitresses called Nippies
(so-called because they were nippy on their
feet), orchestras played to the diners in palatial
rococo-style rooms filled with palm trees.

While the Lyons Corner House did not
survive beyond the 1970s, pushed out by
changing fashions and a preference for
American-style fast foods, other tearooms
survive and flourish. Charles Rennie
Mackintosh's Willow Tea Rooms in Glasgow,
designed in his inimitable style in 1903 and
recently refurbished, is one the city's most
popular eating places today.

TODAY
Coffee, rather than tea, but served
with traditional scones, is the choice
of these visitors to Charles Rennie
Mackintosh's Willow Tea Rooms.

1905
Beatrix Potter at the door of Hill Top, her Lake District home and the setting for many of her delightful children's stories.

NATIONAL TRUST

Among the many organizations in the UK concerned with protecting the environment, the National Trust and the National Trust for Scotland stand out as charities that protect and conserve both buildings of historic interest and areas of natural beauty.

Founded in 1895, the NT acquired its first property, Alfriston Clergy House in Sussex, in 1896. Today, it looks after 667,000 acres (270,000 hectares) of land in England, Wales and Northern Ireland, on which stand 200 historic houses, 160 gardens, 40,000 ancient monuments and archeological remains and 46 villages. Over the border, the National Trust for Scotland has in its care 125 properties and 185,000 acres (75,000 hectares) of land.

To visit a National Trust property is to step into a piece of Britain's heritage. From Hill Top, birthplace of Peter Rabbit and other famous characters created by Beatrix Potter, to spectacular Tyntesfield in Somerset, from Lundy Island in the Bristol Channel to the Farne Islands, there is some part of the nation's history in the NT's devoted care.

TODAY
Beatrix Potter bequeathed Hill Top farm, near Sawry, to the National Trust, which keeps the farm house and its garden exactly as she left it.

THE PUB

The character of the public house, licensed to sell beers and spirits to local people – mostly men – has changed fundamentally in recent decades. A change in drinking habits, begun when men chose to go to working men's clubs rather than to the pub, was accelerated by television, which has tended to keep families at home in the evenings.

There were some 50,500 pubs in the UK at the Millennium, about 6 per cent fewer than in 1990. But pubs still have sales totalling nearly £14 billion in the UK, and many of them are radically changing what they offer in order to attract more customers.

The biggest change that publicans have made is to sell proper food, of an increasingly high standard. Pubs with a theme (Irish is very popular these days), pubs that offer karaoke or DJs on Friday and Saturday nights, quiz evenings and jazz nights all attract the crowds. But there's nothing like watching a big football match in a like-minded crowd, and football on TV is getting people out of their living rooms and into the pub again.

A St Bernard rests after having won
eight awards at Crufts. Its owner has
slipped off her show-ring shoes and
is having a quiet smoke.

CRUFTS

The world's greatest dog show does not need
a long name: everyone knows what Crufts is.
The annual competition, the most important
in the pedigree dog show year, is named after
Charles Cruft, the general manager of James
Spratt, a dog-biscuit manufacturing company.

In 1886, Mr Cruft organized a dog show,
perhaps seeing it as a good way to promote
his company's products. The competition he
began has been held every year since then,
apart from the war years and one or two
others. The 100th Crufts Show was held in
2003, with more than 22,000 dogs from
177 different breeds taking part.

Crufts was a show solely for British dogs
until anti-rabies laws were relaxed. Now dogs
from abroad can take part, provided they have
won qualifying events at home. Dogs compete
in seven major classes for the title Supreme
Champion, take part in obedience classes, and
demonstrate their speed and agility in other
events. Owners and handlers start young:
children from twenty countries helped to
show and handle dogs in the 2003 show.

TODAY
Nord Champion Topscore
Contradiction, a three-year-old
standard poodle from Norway, was
Best in Show at Crufts in 2002.

THE CHANNEL

Until the steamship brought regular services and cheap fares to the business, crossing the Channel was a hazardous and unreliable business dependent on tide, wind and weather.

The steamship made crossing the Channel so much easier that increasing numbers of people, many of them led by travel pioneer Thomas Cook, found their way to Europe. The age of the motor car gave cross-Channel ferries a new problem, overcome by treating cars as freight to be hoisted aboard with the help of a crane. Then came the roll-on, roll-off ferry, revolutionizing the cross-Channel trip for both commercial and holiday traffic.

But nothing has revolutionized cross-Channel travel like the Channel Tunnel. First planned by a Frenchman in 1802, attempted in 1880 and finally realized in 1994, the Channel Tunnel is used by a drive-on, drive-off shuttle train service and by a high-speed passenger service, operated by British, French and Belgian railways. With London only three hours from Paris, no wonder nearly eight million people travel under the Channel every year.

TODAY
A train of the Eurostar Channel Tunnel passenger service makes ready to leave the Waterloo Eurostar Terminal in London.

71

THE MINI

When the first Alec Issigonis-designed Mini car rolled off the production line in 1959 it started a revolution in car ownership. It was the first high-performance small saloon car and, at £469, was within the price reach of many young people, whose earning power was to increase dramatically in the carefree, swinging, Beatles-crazy 1960s.

The Mini wasn't just another small car. It had style, and soon everyone wanted one, or at least to be seen driving along the Kings Road in one – preferably one with wickerwork door panels, like Peter Sellers' Mini. Seeing how many people could be pushed into a Mini outdid stuffing people into telephone boxes as a student craze and half a dozen Minis even starred in a very popular film, *The Italian Job*.

Long after the Swinging Sixties had given way to less carefree times, the Mini continued selling in large numbers, with total sales of five million by the mid-1980s. In 2001, a revamped version of the Mini was produced. It sold well, despite a basic price tag of £10,000.

TODAY
A new Williams BMW Mini on the streets of Manchester during the national launch of the revamped English classic car in 2001.

CARAVANNING

It does not take a large car to tow a caravan, so the motor car opened up new vistas of enjoyable holidays for the British people in the years after World War I. Visits to the countryside or the seaside, with a place to stay already attached to the car, sounded irresistible, especially with the Automobile Association and, later, the Caravan Club able to offer advice and assistance.

British-made Austin and Morris tourers could get about country roads at 30 miles an hour (48 kilometres an hour) and were reliable enough to need only simple repairs that most motorists could do themselves. The caravans they towed were not spacious, but had primus stoves for cooking and offered good shelter from bad weather.

The modern trailer or motor caravan is a very different thing, the grandest offering all the comforts of a hotel. Parked on a good caravan site, the facilities of which could include a swimming pool and tennis courts as well as the more usual shops and laundry facilities, even the simplest caravan offers its owners the chance of a memorable holiday.

TODAY
Everyone, including the dog, is enjoying the sun at a caravan site at Onich, on the shores of Loch Linnhe in the Scottish Highlands.

75

WOMEN GET THE VOTE

Although the move towards parliamentary democracy in Britain began in 1832, with the first Reform Act, by the end of the century women could still see no sign that they would ever be involved in the process.

Mrs Emmeline Pankhurst organized the Women's Social and Political Union in 1905 and led the fight, with increasing violence, for women's suffrage. One way the Union drew attention to the cause was by publishing a newspaper, *Votes for Women*, which carried articles by the principal figures in the campaign, including Mrs Pankhurst and Mrs Emmeline Pethick-Lawrence.

During World War I, women did much of the work that men had done before August, 1914. Their reward was the vote for women over the age of 30, used for the first time in the General Election of December, 1918. Today, all women have the vote and can take a full part in the electoral process.

TODAY

Women manning a polling place in the grounds of a bowling club in Tullibardine, Perthshire, taken over for a Scottish election in 1999.

1931

A young exhibitor arrives at Crystal Palace with her kitten on a harness lead for the National Cat Club's annual show.

CAT FANCIERS' PARADISE

Cat owners have long enjoyed showing off the beauties of their pets. A cat show was included in the attractions of Winchester's St Giles Fair back in 1598. The first modern-style cat show, with benches for showing the cats, took place at the Crystal Palace in London in 1871.

Soon, cat shows were an annual event, organized by the National Cat Club, and the desire to show a favourite cat had reached the highest in the land. Queen Victoria twice entered her pedigree blue Persians in the Cat Club's annual championship show.

The success of cat shows quickly turned selective cat breeding into a serious business. At today's championship shows there are classes for more than a hundred breeds and varieties. One thing has not changed: Queen Victoria's Persian, or Longhair, remains the cat fanciers' favourite. The Longhair is top of the Cat Fanciers' Association's registration list, which is one of the world's biggest.

TODAY

A blue-and-white Cornish Rex gets the full attention of the breed judge and her steward at a recent National Championship Show.

PLEASURE PIERS

'A good pier has long been regarded as an essential to a seaside town,' noted a Brighton guide book in the 1890s. In 1872, Eastbourne, just along the coast from Brighton, got a pier to add to its other amenities. It was designed by the engineer Eugenius Birch, one of the country's most prolific pier designers. In 1888, a pavilion and concert hall were added to the piers amenities, which included an American Bowling Saloon, a Rifle Saloon with Electric Targets, and matinees in the concert hall.

Eastbourne Pier almost became a casualty of war in 1940, when the Army considered blowing it up to prevent it being used by German landing parties. In the end the Army simply removed a section of decking instead.

The pier was refurbished in 1996 and its Victorian splendour recreated, though many of its amenities, including a family amusement centre, nightclub and Waterfront Bar, are very much of the twenty-first century. Eastbourne pier, unlike Birch's West Pier at Brighton, wrecked in a storm followed by fire in 2003, is again a premier South Coast attraction.

TODAY
Sunbathers relax in front of Eastbourne's recently refurbished pier. Later, they will be able to enjoy the pier's evening attractions.

THE TELEPHONE ON THE STREET

When the telephone, patented by Alexander Graham Bell in 1876, was first made available for public use, callers were connected via a telephone exchange. An automatic dialling system, first used in Britain in 1912, made communication by phone much easier.

The General Post Office made the new system available in the street via a standardized design telephone box, introduced in 1921 and complete with dial phone, a coin box for payment and telephone directories. Painted bright red and with a royal crown displayed above the door, the telephone box remained a prominent piece of street furniture until the end of the century.

Declining standards of public behaviour brought about the end of the red telephone kiosk. Vandalized, their telephone books defaced and coin boxes broken into, most kiosks have been replaced by phones with plastic hoods and slots for payment cards.

1938
A policeman has a quiet word with
some boys trying to get a sneak
preview of Bertram Mills Tenting
Circus, in rehearsal at Luton.

THE POLICE

The police force in Britain can trace its origins
back to the Bow Street Runners, a force
created in 1749 by the novelist Henry
Fielding, who was also justice of the peace to
Westminster, in an attempt to suppress the
ruffianly disorder of the times. Prime Minister
Robert Peel built on Fielding's idea in 1829
when he created the London police force. This
was so effective that by 1852 the system was
being introduced throughout the country.

Today, London has two police forces, and
another 50 local forces bring law and order to
the rest of the country. There are also a
National Criminal Intelligence Service, a
National Crime Squad and a Forensic Science
Service to help local forces in their work.

While the business of policing has become
more complex and more dependent on
science and technology than Fielding and Peel
could ever have imagined, the police man and
woman covering their beat every day are still
doing much the same job as the first 'peelers'
or 'bobbies' were doing: keeping the streets
safe and free of crime for everyone.

TODAY
Police officers ready to get on their
bikes while policing a shopping
street in a town in Cumbria.

SPORTS & ENTERTAINMENT 3

MOTOR RACING

Once motor cars became reliable at speed, motor racing took off. The first races were over roads for long periods of time that tested the endurance of car and driver alike.

The world's first special motor course was built at Brooklands, near Weybridge in Surrey, in 1906–7. Here, on a specially banked circuit, the Brooklands Automobile Racing Club and other clubs held races, driving tests, speed trials and long-distance races for sports cars and pure racing cars up to 1939. Circuits built after Brooklands included Donington Park, Brand's Hatch and, after World War II, Silverstone in Northamptonshire, which is today the venue of the British Grand Prix.

The first Grand Prix race was held in France in 1906, and by the 1930s, when Grand Prix races had long been held on closed circuits, pit work on the cars was getting near a fine art.

Today's Grand-Prix racing car's pit team is a miracle of speedy efficiency, with each member as important an element in the car's success as the army of designers, engineers, technicians and drivers who built the car in the first place.

1934

A young Arsenal fan exercises his lungs at the start of a London derby, Arsenal v. Tottenham Hotspur, at Highbury, Arsenal's home since 1913.

FOOTBALL

Association football is Britain's favourite team sport, played and watched by millions. It has inspired best-selling novels, television soap operas, movies, plays and musicals.

The game in the UK today is run by four separate Football Associations, all descended from the Football Association founded in England in 1863. The FA and the Football League, founded in 1888, were both the first organizations of their kind in the world.

When the FA was formed, it had just a dozen or so teams to deal with, most of which were made up of players who worked together, rather than living in the same town. London's Arsenal team, for instance, was made up of workers at the Woolwich Arsenal – hence their nickname, 'the Gunners'.

Today, 314 clubs are affiliated to the FA and about 42,000 clubs are affiliated to regional or district associations. The Scottish FA has 78 full and associate clubs and nearly six thousand registered clubs under its jurisdiction. No longer just a sport, football is very big business indeed and success is vital for a major club's wellbeing.

TODAY

Celtic fans in full voice get their club's colours well to the fore at one of the Glasgow team's home games.

91

DERBY DAY

The Derby, a race for three-year-old colts and fillies, is one of the classics of British flat racing. It was first run at Epsom, even then a fifty-year-old race course, in 1780.

By early in Victoria's reign, the Derby had become more than just another race. It was a highlight of the English racing calendar and a popular day out for the masses, who were able to enjoy all the fun of the fair that took over Epsom Downs for the day. William Frith's *Derby Day*, painted in 1858, captured well the fun and excitement of the occasion.

The Derby lost something of its shine in the last decade or so of the twentieth century. The prize money was less than that offered in other races and fewer people took time off in mid-week to attend. Moving the Derby to a Saturday and increasing the prize money helped return the race to the status of a must-attend event. The hospitality boxes and tents are packed, double-decker buses offer great views for those who come in them and the champagne flows freely. Within a horse-shoe's throw of them all, the bookies win fortunes.

TODAY

Racing fans crowd Epsom Downs on Derby Day. The on-course bookies are ranged along the fence, ready to take the punters' money.

c.1901

Punts and rowing boats crowd
together near the finishing line as
their occupants watch an eights race
at the Henley Regatta.

HENLEY REGATTA

A high point of the year for the sport of
rowing in Britain is the Henley Royal Regatta.
The oldest rowing regatta in Europe and the
most famous in the world, the first Henley
Regatta was held in 1839, 10 years after the
first Oxford and Cambridge Boat Race was
rowed over the reach at Henley-on-Thames.

Throughout Victoria's reign, the Henley
Regatta was a major attraction for rowers and
a high point of the summer social scene.
Rowing clubs, universities and schools, both
the great public schools and schools from
local riverside towns, sent teams to compete
for the various trophies, the oldest of which –
the Grand Challenge Cup, for eights – was
rowed for at the first Henley Regatta.

Today the Regatta, long a major event in the
international rowing calendar, has acquired
added celebrity. It was at the Henley Regatta
that the five-times Olympic Gold Medal
winner Steve Redgrave honed the race-
winning skills that, added to years of practice
on the Thames, enabled him to become the
most successful rower of all time.

TODAY

Olympic Gold Medal winners
Matthew Pinsent, three times Steve
Redrave's Olympic partner, and James
Cracknell win at Henley in 2002.

THE FA CUP

English football has its most glorious day of
the year when the final of the FA (Football
Association) Cup is played. It is the climax of a
knock-out competition involving teams from
all the football divisions – and involving, too,
enough luck to ensure that it is not always the
great teams from the Premier Division who
reach the later stages and even the final.

The first FA Cup final was held in March,
1872, when a crowd of about two thousand
people saw Wanderers beat the Royal
Engineers 1–0 at Kennington Oval. Fifteen
clubs, including Queen's Park, Glasgow, entered
the competition 'for a Challenge Cup open to
all clubs belonging to the Football Association'.

Scotland having long had its own FA Cup,
today's FA Cup final is an all-English affair.
While the strength of, and therefore the main
interest in, English football lies in the week-by-
week programme of the Football League, the
FA Cup knock-out competition retains all its
exciting magic, despite being deprived, albeit
temporarily, of its traditional ground, the
hallowed turf of Wembley Stadium.

TODAY

Arsenal's Fredrik Ljungberg sprays
team-mates and the FA Cup with
champagne after his team defeated
Chelsea to win the 2002 Cup final.

HIGHLAND GAMES

The athletics meetings known as Highland
Games were first held in the highlands of
Scotland early in the nineteenth century.

Similar sports meetings begun at much the
same time, such as those in the Scottish
lowlands (Border Games) and the Lake
District of England (Lakeland Games), have
lost something of their former glory. But the
Highland Games, particularly the famous
Royal Highland Gathering, held every September
at the small Deeside town of Braemar,
continue to be very popular. The Queen and
other members of the Royal Family never miss
attending the Braemar Gathering, if they are in
residence at Balmoral Castle, the royal home
in Scotland, just six miles away.

Most Highland Games are a mixture of
standard track and field events and
competitions with a more cultural flavour, such
as Scottish country dancing and bagpipe
playing. Some peculiarly Scottish events, like
tossing the caber and tossing the weight, add
to visitors' enjoyment of the Games.

TODAY

A competitor attempts to toss the
caber – a tree trunk of unspecified
size – at the Cowal Highland
Gathering in Dunoon, Argyll.

99

1919
Elegantly dressed Ascot race-goers
make their way past ordinary folk
who have no need of expensive
grandstand tickets to enjoy their day.

ROYAL ASCOT

Queen Anne started the Royal Ascot race
meeting at her racecourse near Ascot in 1711.
The racecourse, which is near Windsor Castle,
is one of the finest in the country and remains
in royal hands. So does the organization of the
Royal Ascot meeting, a highlight of the flat
racing season, which takes place in June.

Royal Ascot is today, as it has been since
Edward VII's reign, the highest point of
England's social whirl. It is the Queen's
racecourse and the only one in the country
where she and her family and other guests
arrive by way of a drive in elegant horse-
drawn carriages up the race track.

The quality of the racing is generally
outstanding, too. It is flat racing, under Jockey
Club rules, and the cream of the country's
race horses are entered for the four days of
racing. Among the most important of the races
held during Royal Ascot week is the Ascot
Gold Cup, a race over $2\frac{1}{2}$ miles (4,000 metres)
first run in 1807 and now the highlight of
Ladies Day, when women race-goers put on
their largest and most extravagant hats.

TODAY
Ladies Day at Royal Ascot, when the
women's hats steal the limelight.
Men, in contrast, wear grey toppers
and morning coats.

101

CAR RALLYING

In the early days of car rallying, a sport that included the excitement of driving cars across country in all weathers, the sport was open to everyone. A well-maintained and highly tuned car was the key to success, and even a humble Austin, Morris, Wolseley or Ford could provide a triumphant win in a major event.

As engines became more sophisticated, with electronic controls to increase efficiency and improve performance, keen motorists wanting to take part in the top rallies had to become technically expert too.

Car rallying is a motor sport that everyone with an ordinary car can enjoy – at the level of car club and similar rallies, anyway. At the top level of rallying – such as the Rally of Great Britain – an event in the World Rally Championship in which Britons have excelled in recent years, cars must be highly tuned and their drivers very skilled. The numbers who turn out to watch, in snowy Scottish forests and rain-swept Welsh hill country, attest to the great attraction of a motor sport with which all car drivers can identify.

1930s
Fashions may change for players and
spectators, but the ingredients of
club cricket – tea tent, deck chairs,
the sound of ball on willow – don't.

CRICKET

The quintessentially English game of cricket, a
form of which had been played in England and
other countries for centuries, began in its
modern form in the peaceful village of
Hambledon in Hampshire in the 1760s.
Although much has happened to cricket since,
quiet cricket on village greens and in parks
remains the bedrock of the game.

The centre of the game had moved to
London by the 1790s, when the Marylebone
Cricket Club was formed. The rules of the
game were agreed at the MCC in 1835, and
have changed little in essentials since. Overarm
bowling was allowed after 1864 and the
classification of cricketers into Gentlemen and
Players (with their own dressing rooms at test
matches) was abolished in 1963.

Cricket is a hierarchy of club cricket, county
cricket, one-day cricket and test match cricket.
The last is played between countries
introduced to the game by Victorian empire-
builders sent out to reproduce the English
way of life in their colonial possessions. For
many, cricket is the best legacy of Empire.

TODAY
A giant TV screen displays the
Lord's website name during a test
match between England and
Sri Lanka at Lord's in 2002.

105

1955
John Lennon and the Quarrymen provide the music, complete with a tea-chest-and-broom-handle bass, at St Peter's Church fete, Woolton.

POPULAR MUSIC

A popular music revolution got under way in Britain in the 1950s, strongly influenced by the amazing sounds coming across the Atlantic from such pioneers of rock and roll as Bill Haley, Elvis Presley and Chuck Berry.

Skiffle was an early musical response in Britain to all this, and many teenagers formed their own skiffle groups. Few of them became as famous as John Lennon, whose first group, the Quarrymen, were happy to cut their performing teeth at church fetes and to include in their band a bass made out of a tea-chest, a broom handle and a length of string.

Today, great rock musicians are more likely to be found performing before vast crowds at yet another venue on their latest world tour or in front of equally large and often rain-soaked, mud-caked crowds at music festivals. Kicking off on the Isle of Wight in 1970 and at Glastonbury shortly afterward, the star-studded rock music festival is now an essential part of the British summer scene. Festivals may be simply a case of sex, drugs and rock'n'roll to their elders, but to the young they are musical heaven.

TODAY
The Reading Festival, one of the country's biggest rock music events, gets underway again at Reading in Royal Berkshire.

1907
A throw-in is taken during a rugby game played at the Queen's Club, now better known for its tennis, in west London.

RUGBY

Rugby football gets its name from Rugby School in England, where it is claimed that in 1823 a boy first picked up the ball in a football game and ran with it. Until mid-century, football, as played in most English boys' public and grammar schools, was seen as one game, with variations. Eventually, the differences became annoying, and separate sets of rules were formulated for football and rugby, which itself later divided in union and league forms.

Rugby, taken to the far corners of the world by young Empire-builders from English schools, is more limited in its international appeal than the much less physically violent football. Commonwealth countries such as Australia, New Zealand – home of the fearsome All Blacks – and South Africa provide particularly strong competition for the four home rugby union teams, with Argentina, France, Italy and others adding spice to the international game.

Both union and league rugby are strong sports in Britain today, played by hundreds of men (and rather fewer women) in both amateur and professional competitions.

TODAY
Scotland's Mattie Stewart runs with the ball in a match against France at Murrayfield during the 2002 Six Nations Championship.

MARATHON RUNNING

The marathon is the longest race to figure in major athletics championships. It gets its name from the story of Phidippides, a Greek soldier who ran from the Battle of Marathon to Athens, 22 miles away, with the message of the Greeks' victory over the Persians.

When the first Olympic Games of the modern era were held in 1896, a marathon race was naturally included. Set at 26 miles, it had an extra 385 yards added in 1908 so that the competitors, having run from Windsor to London, would end up opposite the Royal Box in the White City Stadium.

Today, Londoners can watch a great marathon every year. The London Marathon, first organized by Olympic Gold Medal winner Chris Brasher in 1981, is today the world's biggest marathon. It draws the cream of the world's long-distance runners, plus thousands of amateurs running for personal satisfaction and to raise money for good causes.

TODAY

Paula Radcliffe won the 2002 Women's London Marathon, in a new course record of 2:18:56 (In 2003, she broke the record again!).

TIMEX®

FLORA LONDON MARATHON 2002

MUSIC

Music moved out of private drawing rooms
and exclusive concert halls to find a much
wider audience in Victorian Britain. Interest in
music was encouraged by the growth of nonconformist Christianity – its large chapels
made superb concert halls, ideal for the singing
of choral works such as Handel's *Messiah* and
Haydn's *Creation* and by the thriving life of
municipalities, whose grand town halls usually
included a large auditorium for concerts and
choral performances.

Open-air band concerts, performed from the
shelter of bandstands that were a feature of
the new public parks and seaside pleasure
gardens, became a regular part of many
families' Sunday afternoons.

The great tradition of Victorian public music-
making, particularly orchestral music and the
oratorio singing fostered by English and Welsh
choral societies, lives on the UK. Perhaps its
most joyously uninhibited time comes amidst
the carnival atmosphere of the last night of the
Promenade Concerts that the BBC holds in
the Royal Albert Hall, London, every summer.

COWES

The small town of Cowes, Britain's yachting 'capital', lies on the Isle of Wight facing the Solent, the fine stretch of water between the Isle of Wight and the southern coast of England. Every August the town is crowded with yachtsmen and their gear, come to take part in Cowes Week, the biggest of the many yachting regattas that take place round Britain's coasts every summer.

Among the most famous of the races connected with Cowes is the Round-the-Island race every June and the Fastnet Race, from Cowes to the Fastnet Rock and back, held every two years.

The America's Cup began as a race for a trophy presented by the Royal Yacht Squadron in 1851 for a race round the Isle of Wight. The race was won by an American yacht, the *America*, which gave its name to the trophy. It was over a century before the America's Cup was wrested from the Americans, going to the Antipodes for several series of Cup races. In 2003 the America's Cup was won by a Swiss syndicate and thus returned to Europe.

1939

There is a good crowd near the track-side bookies' stands for this greyhound race meeting, but the crowds are sparse elsewhere.

GOING TO THE DOGS

Greyhound racing as a sport in England was mentioned in the fifteenth-century *Boke of St Albans*, but seems to have died out. Modern greyhound racing, in which dogs chase a mechanical hare round a track, came to Britain from America, where the first track was opened in 1919.

Britain's first greyhound racing track was built at Bellevue in Manchester in 1926 and soon after that the rules of greyhound racing were laid down. The National Greyhound Racing Club now administers them.

In its early days, greyhound racing found its largest numbers of supporters among working people. Today, it is one of Britain's most popular spectator sports, with about four million people going to the dogs every year at 32 major tracks and about the same number of smaller independent ones. The high spot of the greyhound racing year is the Greyhound Derby, run in June at Wimbledon Stadium.

TODAY

Diners can enjoy the racing without leaving their tables in the Stowaway Grill Restaurant at the Walthamstow greyhound track.

1865
A golfer makes ready to putt at the
Royal and Ancient Gold Club,
St Andrews. There are no golf bags,
so caddies carry the clubs underarm.

GOLF

The modern game of golf developed in
Scotland in the eighteenth century out of a
game the Scots had played for centuries. Mary,
Queen of Scots, was a keen player and her
son, James VI (James I of England), took the
game to England, although it did not really
catch on south of the border until late in the
nineteenth century.

Golfers from a new club at St Andrews, later
the Royal and Ancient Golf Club, drew up for
their inaugural competition in 1754 the first
written rules to have survived. Today, the Royal
and Ancient Golf Club of St Andrews
administers the rules of golf worldwide, except
in the USA and Mexico, and the rules they
administer are infinitely more complex than
the thirteen they started with in 1754.

Golfers have a choice of over two thousand
courses on which to play the game in the UK
today. The amateur game long ago opened its
doors to women, whose golf is governed by
the Ladies Golf Union. For every lover of the
game, the highlight of the golfing year is the
Open Championship, one of the world's four
'major' events.

TODAY
It's the Weetabix Women's British
Open at Sunningdale Golf Club,
Surrey in 2001, and Trish Johnson of
England lines up a putt.

119

1955
A state occasion at Covent Garden. The Queen, the President of Portugal and their suites arrive for a performance of *The Bartered Bride*.

OPERA FOR ALL

There has been an opera house in London's Covent Garden since 1732, and the present building is the third one on the site. Until World War II it was privately owned and presented seasons of opera and ballet to largely rich and aristocratic audiences.

After 1945, when the Royal Opera House re-opened as a public company and was given a state subsidy, its audiences changed, in line with the social changes that were taking place in Britain. Black tie and evening dress, essential in 1946, had given way to jeans and T-shirts (in the stalls as well as the gallery) by 1997, when the Opera House closed for a controversial and very expensive refit.

In its handsomely rebuilt and much more welcoming new form, the Royal Opera House is still devoted to its core ideal of presenting opera and ballet to world-class standards. But this is an expensive business and publicly funded organizations must not seem elitist. A giant screen in the Piazza is one of several ways in which the Royal Opera House makes its productions more accessible to everyone.

TODAY
Hearing Placido Domingo for free. A performance in the Royal Opera House is shown on a giant screen in the Covent Garden Piazza.

SAILING

The British, called 'an island race' so often it is almost a cliché, nevertheless have a special relationship with the sea. The poet John Masefield called it 'sea fever', and wrote that 'the call of the running tide ... is a clear call that may not be denied'.

At the 2000 Olympic Games, the British team demonstrated this special relationship by winning five medals, making Britain the most successful nation in the sailing events.

Where 'sailing' once meant simply being at sea in a craft with a sail, today it is a broad term covering yacht and dinghy sailing, powerboat racing, motor cruising, jet skiing and windsurfing on inland and offshore waters. One of the main aims of sailing's national body, the Royal Yachting Association, is to make all forms of boating as accessible as possible.

From club moorings and harbour jetties, from river mouths, beaches and rocky shores all round the coast, nearly eight million men and women launch themselves on to waters in and around Britain every year in pursuit of their favourite form of sailing.

1921

The Nottingham Goose Fair is in full swing, and the crowds enjoy the wide range of attractions and entertainments on offer.

FUN AT THE FAIR

Many of the fairs held round the United Kingdom every year are descendants of the great markets and fairs that were established by royal charter from medieval times for the sale of a wide range of foods and goods or for the hiring of labour. Some can trace their beginnings to Saxon times.

Nottingham's Goose Fair, three days of fun and merrymaking every October, was established by a charter of Edward I as an annual fair for the selling of geese and other goods. Thousands of geese were driven to the fair, their feet treated with tar and sand to help them cover the many miles from as far away as Lincolnshire and Norfolk.

Geese ceased to be the major reason for the Nottingham Goose Fair long ago and by the nineteenth century people were going to it just for the merrymaking. Today, Goose Fair is a national institution, and one of the biggest annual fun fairs in the country. Its opening is proclaimed by the town clerk with full traditional ceremony, involving the Lord Mayor and the Sheriff of Nottingham.

TODAY

A brilliantly lit helter-skelter dominates the Nottingham Goose Fair, still one of the great attractions in the Midlands every year.

COUNTRY LIFE **4**

c.1914

Target shooting practice with a difference. Three men and a dog in a boat, rat shooting on the Norfolk Broads.

FIELD SPORTS

Field sports in the UK include hunting, shooting, stalking, ferreting, falconry and hare coursing. Country people have followed them all for centuries, in the past more for survival than for sport. Today, shooting is the favourite field sport for thousands of men and women in all parts of the country.

Not all shooting is for live birds or game. Clay pigeon, or trap, shooting, and skeet, which grew out of sportsmen's desire to have all-year-round shooting practice, quickly became very popular sports in their own right. Clay-shooting schools are increasing in number all over the UK.

Game bird shooting seasons are strictly controlled in the UK, to protect bird populations and their breeding seasons. The grouse shooting season, for instance, starts on August 12, long known as 'the Glorious Twelfth'. From then until early December, butts on the grouse moors of Scotland are filled with sportsmen and women seeking, often at considerable expense, to shoot hundreds of birds a day.

TODAY

Enjoying the start of the grouse shooting season from a butt on the Moy Estate near Inverness in Scotland.

1949

The housewives of Olney, aprons flying, come into the home straight on their annual pancake race.

SPECIAL EVENTS

Hundreds of traditional customs and ceremonies that can be traced back centuries are re-enacted in Britain every year. Many of them are calendar customs – that is, they fall on the same date every year. Others are seasonal or their dates vary because they are connected to Easter, which is a moveable feast.

Pancake races are run by women on Shrove Tuesday, the last chance for letting off steam before Lent begins. The most famous of them is the Olney Pancake Race, which was first run through the village of Olney, in Buckinghamshire, in the mid-fifteenth century. It lapsed in Victorian times in the face of the vicars' disapproval, and was revived in its present form in 1947.

Since the fifteenth century, large round Double Gloucester cheeses have been rolled down the two-in-one slope of Cooper's Hill, near Gloucester, in May (today, this takes place on the Spring bank holiday). The cheeses are pursued in turn by men, women, boys and girls and the winner of each race wins a cheese.

Today

Another running of the annual cheese-rolling competition down Cooper's Hill, near Gloucester.

MARKETS DAYS

For centuries, livestock and food markets in towns and villages were the main outlets for farmers' cattle and produce. Market day might have been a day for doing business, but it was also a social occasion, and a time for meeting friends over pints of ale in the market tavern.

Changing trading patterns and transport systems, and more stringent health laws, caused livestock markets to be merged on sites away from town centres. While general markets still flourish, most of us today buy our food at supermarkets, where much of what is on the fresh food shelves gets there long after it leaves the farm it was grown on.

To met the growing demand for fresh, organically grown food, farmers have started bringing their own food to town again. Farmers' markets have become the only place in town, from Islington and Pimlico in London to Aberystwyth and Hexham, for buying fresh meat, fruit and vegetables, unpasteurized cheeses, venison sausages, and a lot more. There is even a fully fledged National Association of Farmers' Markets to oversee their work.

133

1925
Winston Churchill (right), aged 50, was a member of the House of Commons polo team that defeated the Lords at Ranelagh.

POLO

A Persian poet described the game of polo as long ago as 600BC, and it had long been played in India when the British, especially army men, discovered the fast and furious horseback game in the 1850s, played it with enthusiasm and brought it back to England.

As in India, the strongest supporter of polo in England was the Army, and it was two leading regiments, the 9th Lancers and 10th Hussars, who contested the first polo match at Hounslow, near London, in 1871.

The American Gordon Bennett, who financed H M Stanley's expedition to find David Livingstone in Africa, introduced polo into the United States, and by 1914 the game was known throughout the world.

Today, polo in Britain is still very much a game played by the well-off and by teams of players from the armed services. It is also played by members of the Royal Family, often on the polo grounds in Windsor Great Park. Royal participation increases public interest, and when Prince William took up the game, it rose again in popularity as a spectator sport.

TODAY
The Emerging and Black Bears teams contest the final of the Veuve Clicquot Gold Cup for polo at Cowdray Park, West Sussex, in 2002.

COUNTRY CRAFTS

Although farming in Britain is a highly mechanized business, many old crafts and skills, once essential to maintaining a farm's land and buildings in good condition, are still practised today. Some, like thatching and hedge-laying, are no longer vitally important in modern countryside management but are kept going by organizations such as the Countryside Agency because they provide such strong links with the country's past.

Other crafts are still a part of everyday life in many parts of Britain. Go to County Armagh in Northern Ireland or to Sutherland and Strathspey in the far north of Scotland and you will find people cutting precisely sized turfs from the peat bogs for winter fuel.

In Welsh slate quarries, slate is split and prepared to makes roofing tiles. And in many upland districts of Britain, such as the Derbyshire Peak District and the Yorkshire Moors, stone from the land provides material for dry stone walls that shelter stock and withstand for decades the wind and weather that would rapidly destroy hedges and fences.

TODAY

A splendid vista of dry stone walls marking field boundaries in the Derbyshire Peak District.

1936
Climbers enjoy the view from a snow-capped ridge in Snowdonia, today at the heart of one of Wales' three national parks.

NATIONAL PARKS

The idea of establishing national parks in Britain grew out of a fear that too much of the countryside was being lost to industry and the spread of urbanization and, at the same time, that too few people were able to enjoy the beauty of Britain's lovely land. National parks, established by an act of parliament in 1949, are areas of countyside where the landscape, biodiversity and recreational resources are recognized as having national importance.

The country's first national park was the Peak District National Park, mainly in Derbyshire but extending into surrounding counties, which was established in 1951. It was soon followed by the Lake District National Park in Cumbria and the Snowdonia National Park, covering 838 square miles (2,180 square kilometres) of wild and beautiful country in Gwynedd, North Wales, with the Snowdon massif at its heart.

Today there are eight national parks in England, three in Wales and one in Scotland, each containing countryside of great natural beauty and extraordinarily diverse ranges of flora and fauna.

TODAY
Beautiful Loch Lomond is at the heart of the Loch Lomond and Trossachs National Park, Scotland's first such park, established in 2002.

1936
The 'Costume' race, with riders in fancy dress, underway at the Haywards Heath Horticultural Society's Summer show.

EQUESTRIAN EVENTS

The steam and combustion engines may have ended the horse's essential part in transport, but it still plays a major role in people's leisure activities, especially in the country.

The late nineteenth and early twentieth centuries saw a blossoming of many kinds of equestrian competition. Some of them, like point-to-points, involved races across country, and others, like show jumping, took place in show rings at agricultural shows. Between the wars, horse-riding and the many events associated with it flourished, with many Pony Clubs helping to train children to become the competitive riders of the future.

Competing with show-jumping in popularity today, with both competitors and spectators, is the Three-Day Event, or Horse Trials. This supreme form of horse competition, held over three days, tests the all-round ability of horse and rider by way of dressage; speed, endurance and cross-country; and show jumping.

TODAY
Taking a fence in the cross-country phase of the Gatcombe Park Horse Trials, held each year at the country home of the Princess Royal.

c.1930
Hounds lead the way as a hunt
moves off from its gathering place in
front of a Tudor house in the village
of Eynsford, Kent.

FOX-HUNTING

Hunting has long been a traditional country
activity. Organized fox-hunting, which began in
the eighteenth century, soon became a regular
part of the winter scene, especially in those
Midlands counties, such as Leicestershire,
where the rolling fields and scattered pockets
of woodland made ideal hunting country.

Oscar Wilde may have crisply summarized
fox-hunting as 'the unspeakable in full pursuit
of the uneatable', but for most people riding to
hounds has meant being able to gallop across
country and face up to and overcome the
challenges posed by ditches, hedges, fences and
stone walls.

Fox-hunting in modern Britain is not such a
carefree experience. Modern farming practice,
which involves knocking down fences and
grubbing out hedges to make room for giant
farm machinery, has radically altered much of
the rural landscape. At the same time, a
vociferous anti-hunt lobby has succeeded in
achieving the banning of hunting with dogs in
Scotland, and has caused the government to
consider doing the same in England.

TODAY
A hunt member jumps a ditch in
Berkshire. Modern 'prairie-style'
farming offers riders fewer hedges
and fences for a thrilling ride.

HORSE POWER ON THE FARM

Handsome heavy horses once provided most of the power needed to work farmland, pulling ploughs, harrows and drills. They symbolized the endless toil and ceaseless care that went into creating the British farming landscape.

Heavy horses still work in Britain, often in small, enclosed areas and woodland where machinery is too large to use. But for most of us, the only connection we have today with these magnificent creatures is the horse brasses from their collars and harness that decorate the bars of country pubs or find their way into antique and bric-a-brac shops.

When horse power came to mean the power in the engines of farm machinery, farming changed radically, especially in those areas where crop-growing was paramount. Fewer people now worked in agriculture, and hundreds of miles of centuries-old hedgerows were torn out to make large fields that the great machinery could manoeuvre in.

1938
A line of farm carts makes a good grandstand for spectators at a point-to-point held at Green Street Green, near Farnborough in Kent.

POINT-TO-POINTS

Point-to-point races are said to have grown out of the original form of steeplechasing – races from one point in the countryside to another, usually marked by the steeples of nearby churches, which were first contested in Ireland.

Point-to-point racing in Britain began as an offshoot of hunting. Races are restricted to amateur riders on horses that have qualified by being ridden regularly over the hunting season. The point-to-point season, which includes several Championship and Cup events, is between January and June – several weeks longer than it was thirty years ago, an indication of the increasing popularity of the sport.

Early point-to-points were run straight across country, hence their name. Today, most of the more than one hundred point-to-point tracks are oval, with fences built much the same way as those on ordinary race-courses. Many point-to-point courses are on farming land. The possible banning of fox-hunting in England (it is already banned in Scotland) may change the rules of point-to-point racing, but not its popularity among riders and spectators.

TODAY
Bookmakers first operated on British race courses on Sundays in 1995. These bookies are at a meeting of the Tweseldown Point-to-Point.

CHURCH FETES

A conscientious Victorian vicar or rector and his wife, spending most if not all their time in their country parish, could fill much of their day visiting the old, sick and disabled, overseeing and even teaching at the village's church school, or holding adult education classes in the vicarage.

In our own, more affluent times, the state has taken over many of these responsibilities and church-goers need be less concerned with the problems and needs of the poor at home than with those in third world countries. For them, the country church remains a very active and often architecturally beautiful centre of Christian worship as well as a focal point of village social life.

Today, as in Victorian times, the country church fete – with its beer and tea tent, home-made cake and embroidery stalls, bran tub for the children and games for everyone – remains a high point in the local social calendar, as well as an important source of funds for the upkeep of the church.

TODAY
The vicarage garden at the Anglican church in Boxford, Suffolk, is large enough to hold a big tent and the stalls for the annual church fete.

STAYING IN THE COUNTRY

The railway and the motor car changed the city dweller's attitude to the country. While the Edwardian upper classes perfected the art of the country house weekend, everyone else who had a car or a motorcycle began to discover the delights of country inns, hitherto used to provide a night's food and a bed for relatively few coach travellers.

Country inns, often simple places, were soon upgrading their facilities and putting in extra bathrooms and lavatories. Others joined in the business, so that offering 'bed and breakfast' became a valuable source of extra income for many in country villages and on farms.

Today, the country holiday, promoted by tourist authorities and local councils, can mean bed and breakfast in a country pub, self-catering in a remote farm cottage, or being pampered in a luxurious country house hotel. They all make great holidays and are invaluable revenue earners for the countryside.

TODAY
Time for a chat outside the George Inn at Bathampton, near Bath, where sawn-off lengths of tree trunk provide the drinks tables.

151

CHANGING CITY **5**

1925
Another great ship, RMSP *Asturias*, leaves the slipway after its launch at Belfast docks on July 7.

BELFAST

Back in the nineteenth century, Belfast was one of the fastest-growing cities in the British Isles as it developed its ship-building and engineering industries. At the huge Harland and Wolff Shipyard many of the world's great liners, including the White Star Line's *Titanic*, were built and launched.

The development of the jet engine, which made long-haul flights possible, meant the end of the great days of the ocean liner and also severely damaged merchant shipping. Belfast's glory days were over, the dockyard cranes no longer dominated Belfast's waterfront skyline and shipyards closed. After this disaster, Northern Ireland also endured terrible years of virtual civil war that polarized society.

There is a new spirit abroad in Belfast today, and an optimism that is everywhere expressed in a large rebuilding programme. One of the finest of the new buildings in Belfast is the Waterfront Hall, described as 'a fresh, Modernist take on the Albert Hall', the curved glass frontage of which is very different to the cranes that once lined the waterfront.

TODAY
Concert-goers at Belfast's splendid Waterfront Hall, opened in 1997, have a fine view of the River Lagan from the hall's entrance foyers.

1936

The castle and cathedral at Durham, seen here from Framwellgate Bridge over the River Wear, has dominated the city skyline since medieval times.

CATHEDRAL CITIES

The great Norman cathedral at Durham, towering over the city on its high rock and surrounded on three sides by the River Wear, helps make the city one of the most visually attractive in Britain and certainly the most dramatic of the country's cathedral cities.

A cathedral is a church that is also the seat of a diocesan bishop and does not necessarily have to be large and imposing. Its presence can confer cathedral city status on quite small places. St Asaph Cathedral in north Wales, for instance, is very small and its 'city' is little more than a village. In contrast, St Paul's in London, Canterbury, Exeter and others are at the heart of very great cities.

Britain's cathedrals, most of them built at a time when the Church played a major role in the government of the country, remain important centres of Christian worship today. They are also places of great cultural importance and architectural gems that have inspired generations of artists.

TODAY

It may look as if little has changed in Durham, but beyond the city walls, University buildings are showplaces of modern architecture.

ENGLAND'S NEWEST CITY

There are 66 urban areas in the United Kingdom – 50 of them in England, six in Scotland, five in Wales and five in Northern Ireland – that have been granted city status, a great mark of distinction.

Although a town may think it has all the attributes of a city, only the sovereign, on the advice of her ministers, can grant city status.

Three towns, Brighton and Hove and Wolverhampton in England and Inverness in Scotland, were granted city status in 2000 to mark the Millennium.

England's latest city is Preston, a busy industrial and university city in Lancashire, famed in the nineteenth century for its cotton mills. Preston was one of five UK towns granted city status in 2002, to mark the Queen's Golden Jubilee. Competition for the honour was keen, but nobody denied that Preston, birthplace of Richard Arkwright who invented the spinning jenny, was a worthy recipient of it.

1920s

There are still flower girls on the steps round Eros in Piccadilly Circus, but judging by the already heavy traffic, they will be moving on soon.

PICCADILLY CIRCUS

Although London's central point for measuring the distance to other places is at Charing Cross, Piccadilly Circus has always felt like the centre of town. Once, it was the 'heart of empire' and until World War II the Circus and the streets off it were where London's most fashionable and stylish theatres, restaurants and nightclubs were to be found.

Gentlemen in top hat and tails could stroll across to the flower 'girls' gathered round the Eros fountain, erected in 1893 as a memorial to the philanthropic Lord Shaftesbury, to buy a buttonhole for themselves or flowers for their theatre or dinner companion.

There is not much leisurely strolling done in Piccadilly Circus these days. There is too much traffic and the air is heavy with petrol fumes and cooking smells from fast food eating places. Pedestrians are penned behind railings while they wait for the green light that lets them make a quick dash to the safety of a distant pavement. This is one place where 'yesterday' was preferable to 'today'.

TODAY

The latest traffic-flow scheme around Piccadilly Circus has widened Eros' pavement and placed iron railings around it.

LONDON'S MARKETS

Shopping at market stalls in the street was the norm in the poor districts of London from the nineteenth century up to World War II. Cheap food and clothing were the most essential goods for the low-paid workers who crowded into the run-down housing near the markets. Much of this housing was medieval in origin, while other areas grew up to feed the needs of immigrant populations fleeing persecution, such as the Huguenots and Jews.

The changing ethnic mix of London's population has changed the character, but not the liveliness and vibrancy, of London's street markets. Brick Lane, in Shoreditch, began as a fruit and vegetable market in the eighteenth century and now has many Asian stallholders and shoppers. Brixton, in south London, is the place to go to find the fruits and vegetables essential for good West Indian cooking. And Petticoat Lane, its Sunday opening indicating its Jewish origins, offers something for everyone.

TODAY

Clothes are still a big draw at Petticoat Lane Market, crowded every Sunday with shoppers of many ethnic groups.

Fire-watchers on the roof saved
St Paul's Cathedral from the bombs
that destroyed much of the City of
London in World War II.

ST PAUL'S IN WAR & PEACE

Every great city needs a focus for its pride and
self-belief. Sir Christopher Wren's great
masterpiece in the City of London, St Paul's
Cathedral, provides such a focus for Londoners.
St Paul's was built after the Great Fire of
London destroyed the old cathedral in 1666.
Nearly three hundred years later, the cathedral
survived a far more devastating series of fires,
the result of the Blitz of World War II.

In 1941, pictures of the dome of St Paul's
rising undamaged through the smoke and fire
of the Blitz did almost as much as Winston
Churchill's stirring speeches to maintain
morale and confidence on the Home Front.

St Paul's remains a focus of national pride,
most recently during the celebrations for
Elizabeth II's Golden Jubilee. An exciting new
view of the dome and south side of St Paul's
was opened up for Londoners when a
pedestrian walk down to the new Millennium
Bridge was built over the Thames.

TODAY

Unchanged in the midst of change,
the great dome of St Paul's
Cathedral rises above surrounding
buildings and the streams of traffic.

1937
The Muslim community in Wales forms a procession through the streets of Cardiff as part of the El Elbekir religious ceremony.

THE CHANGING ETHNIC MIX

Perhaps because its early history involved the settling on its lands of so many culturally diverse peoples, Britain has always given a sympathetic, if sometimes muted, welcome to outsiders coming in search of a better life.

Whether they are Huguenots fleeing from religious persecution in France, Jews escaping the horrors of Nazi Germany, or men and women from many of Britain's former imperial possessions, most immigrants have chosen to live in the big cities. This has given many British cities an extraordinarily vibrant cultural and ethnic diversity.

Among the longest-term 'newcomers' are Muslim people. There has been a Muslim community in Britain since the sixteenth century and today their faith, Islam, is the most common in Britain after Christianity. More than a third of British Muslims live in London and many more live in the cities of the West Midlands. Their community in Wales, mostly in Cardiff, is much smaller.

TODAY
A British-Yemeni boy is given instruction on the finer points of the Qur'an at the South Wales Islamic Centre mosque in Cardiff.

167

TRANSPORT IN THE CITY

Because the early railway was not ideal for urban transport, the first mass moving of people round towns and cities was by double-decker, horse-drawn omnibus.

The first omnibus route in London opened in 1829 and by the 1860s omnibuses were carrying 40 million passengers a year. Other big cities could boast similar numbers. By the end of the century horse-drawn omnibuses were being replaced by petrol-driven ones.

Urban railways went underground in 1863, with the construction of the Metropolitan Line in London and two decades later urban tramways turned electric, the first electric trams running in Blackpool in 1885.

Trams and light railways, which do not generate as much pollution as buses, are back in fashion in Britain's cities today. The 1990s saw tram and light railway systems opening from London's Docklands and Croydon to Birmingham, Manchester and Newcastle.

TODAY
Manchester's Metrolink, officially opened in 1992, is Britain's first modern street-operating light rail system.

169

c.1900

Sailing ships and steam freighters are moored closely together in the crowded West India Docks on the Thames in East London.

LONDON'S DOCKLANDS

Until the eve of World War II, the Thames below London Bridge was always crowded with ships from Britain's worldwide empire unloading their goods. Ships that could not find a berth on the river were moved into specially built docks, known by their trading regions – such as the West India Docks and the East India Docks – or given royal names.

London's docklands was a very picturesque quarter, the masts and riggings of the ships and the dockside cranes providing a backdrop for an area teeming with cosmopolitan life. Chinatown had the best Chinese restaurants in England – and the most opium dens.

A thriving new city, still called Docklands, has taken over the docks today. Towering office buildings rise above smart riverside housing, pubs, stylish restaurants and shops. In the old docks, cabin cruisers, sailing boats and floating restaurants bob on the waters once filled with the shipping of a great empire.

TODAY

Canary Wharf Tower, situated in the heart of what used to be London's Docklands, is one of the tallest office blocks in Europe.

171

1858

The towers of York Minster loom over carriages in the sidings at York railway station, built just inside the ancient walls of the city.

HISTORIC YORK

Ironically – given its present troubles with flooding, supposedly caused by global warming – the Romans chose York as a site for its fortress of Eburacum because it was very dry.

After the Romans came the Danes, who founded a colony here, then the Normans. who built massive fortifications of their own, including great walls, built partly on Roman foundations. Real prosperity came to York with the medieval wool trade, much of the profits of which went – over two and a half centuries – into the building of York's magnificent Minster, seat of the Archbishop of York, and which has been called 'a poem in stone'.

Today, York within its city walls is virtually, as King George VI once remarked, a living museum of English history from Roman times, via the Danes – the Jorvic Centre, about Viking life, is a big draw – to the present day. Its Castle Museum and Heritage Centre are other attractions that help bring thousands of visitors to York every year. Outside the medieval walls, York is home to the National Railway Museum.

TODAY

Flowerbeds give splashes of colour to the lawns beneath York's city walls. Only the trappings of traffic control hint that this is present-day York.

ARCHITECTURE AND THE CITY

In the 1960s, Birmingham's Bull Ring became a prime example of what can go wrong when city planners decide to bulldoze the old centres of their cities and recreate them in 'modern' style.

Many British cities had huge problems of urban rebuilding and regeneration after World War II. But in too many of them, the arrival of the bulldozer meant the replacing of old city centres and domestic housing with a concrete, high-rise architecture so stark and so riddled with wind tunnels and exposed walkways that 'brutalism' seemed an apt name for it indeed.

In the 1990s, Birmingham, already brimming with the cultural self-confidence of a city possessing a major symphony orchestra, a leading ballet company and a superb exhibition centre, embarked on a modernization programme that is restoring it to its place as one of Britain's finest cities. The city's current £6 billion 10-year re-development plan for its East Side includes a gleaming new public library.

TODAY
This aerial view of the heart of Birmingham, round the Bull Ring, shows the scale of the rebuilding being undertaken there.

TYNESIDERS

The River Tyne in the north-east of England separates two great metropolitan areas. Newcastle upon Tyne, a cathedral and university city on the river's north bank, is a major ship-building and marine engineering centre. Gateshead, on the south side of the river, is a rapidly growing cultural, sporting and shopping centre for the region.

The two are working together to spearhead the regeneration of the Tyneside region, with a large investment in culture. Being made European City of Culture worked for Glasgow in 1990, and Newcastle-Gateshead, with their bid to be the British candidate for the title of European Capital of Culture in 2008, hope it will work for them.

'Newcastle-Gateshead Buzzin' is the image being projected for the bid. There is plenty buzzing along the Tyne to support the image, from the BALTIC Centre for Contemporary Arts on the Tyne in Gateshead to the amazing Millennium Bridge, assembled at a Tyneside shipyard and lifted into position over the river by one of the world's largest floating cranes.

TODAY
The Gateshead Millennium Bridge, completed in 2001, is the world's first rotating bridge and opens in a 'blinking eye' movement.

Crossing Oxford Street near Selfridges department store was a relaxed business when there were large gaps between the traffic.

OXFORD STREET & THE CAR

When motor vehicles first replaced horse-drawn carriages on city streets such as London's Oxford Street, the advantages were great. Hundreds of tons of stinking horse droppings no longer had to be swept off the streets, car ownership was relatively low and pedestrians still had the advantage in streets. This was an important consideration for shopping streets such as Oxford Street, which already had 153 shops along it in 1800 and by mid-century could boast its first department stores.

The consumer boom saw the relationship between the city and the car deteriorate badly. Drivers demanded wider, people-free roads and somewhere to park their cars in the city. Pollution rose, often to dangerous levels, and traffic jams became the norm. Oxford Street's answer was to ban private cars from much of its length. In 2003, it began to enjoy the benefits of the Mayor of London's Congestion Charge, an experiment that is being watched with interest by city planners everywhere.

TODAY

Traffic streams past Selfridges, stopped only by traffic lights worked by pedestrians penned in by railings in the middle of Oxford Street.

1953

It's Saturday night in Glasgow and crowds throng the intersection of Hope Street and Sauchiehall Street in the centre of the city.

GLASGOW

The great Scottish comedian Harry Lauder used to sing about Glasgow belonging to him, rather than he to the city, after a drink or two on a Saturday night. That was when Glasgow, Scotland's second city, still had a great ship-building industry along the River Clyde and the prosperity that went with it.

The destruction of large parts of the Clyde ship-building docks during World War II, followed by the collapse of the ship-building industry, meant that Glasgow had to pick itself up, dust itself down and start all over again.

Glasgow's appointment as European City of Culture in 1990 spurred the city on to greater efforts to revitalize its flagging economy. In the 1990s the city replaced its almost vanished imperial-age industries with something very different: culture and shopping. Glasgow today has a vibrant theatre life, a new Royal Concert Hall, superb art galleries and a new Museum of Education. These, and the fact that Glasgow is now Britain's second-biggest shopping city, attracts thousands of visitors. Harry Lauder would be proud to belong to Glasgow today.

TODAY

Outwardly not much changed, Glasgow's Hope Street/Sauchiehall Street crossroads is today part of Britain's second-biggest shopping city.

EVERYDAY LIVING **6**

1920s

A boatload of men and women is rowed over the narrow stretch of water to Skye from the mainland at the Kyle of Lochalsh.

OVER THE SEA TO SKYE

The beautiful, mountainous Isle of Skye, off the west coast of Scotland, is celebrated for its place in the story of Bonnie Prince Charlie's escape from the disaster of Culloden in 1746. He made the hazardous journey disguised as Flora Macdonald's maid 'over the sea to Skye' from Benbecula, in the Outer Hebrides.

Had he gone from the mainland, there would have been no story, for the crossing is little more than a stone's throw. The narrow crossing from the Kyle of Lochalsh to Kyleakin on Skye was made by motor boat or car ferry until 1995, when a road bridge was opened.

The new bridge was a toll bridge, and the people of Skye had no choice but to pay its high tolls to get themselves and their sheep and cattle to the mainland because the car ferry service was withdrawn and other island services only ran during the summer. The arguments about paying tolls, and the island's perceived loss of independence, rumble on.

TODAY

The Skye Road Bridge may be a handsome piece of engineering, but it does not please all residents of the Isle of Skye.

SHOPPING

Proprietors of small shops began to feel the
draught from multiple retailers long before
today's supermarkets. As more and more
goods arrived in Victorian Britain from the far-
flung corners of the Empire, far-sighted
retailers began to expand what they sold in
their shops. Then they began adding to the
number of shops they owned. Thomas Lipton,
Marks and Spencer, WH Smith and Boots all
became familiar names on the high street.

Even so, the pattern of shopping in Britain
remained very much that of small shopkeepers
set side-by-side along a town's recognized
shopping streets until the 1950s.

This was the decade in which developers
began tearing down town centres and putting
large, inelegant shopping centres in their place.
Self-service supermarkets, time payment and
shoppers' saving schemes made the spending
of rising wages easier. Then came the out-of-
town shopping mall, depending largely on
almost universal car ownership for its success.
Small shopkeepers were not exactly doomed,
but their numbers dropped drastically.

1913

Men and women on the march for the National Union of Clerks wear masks to prevent victimization by their employers.

TRADE UNIONS

Workers in the first factories of Britain's industrial revolution had no rights. They took the miserable pay and worked the long hours the factory owners chose. The story of British labour relations in the nineteenth century is the story of the growth of the trade union movement and the gradual legal recognition of workers' rights and of their unions in such acts as the Trade Union Act of 1871.

The Labour Party won its first seats in Parliament in 1906, thus giving trade unions a political voice which they used to great effect to improve the lot of their members immeasurably. At the same time, union power got out of hand. Many unions were restrictive and dictatorial, insisting that all workers should belong to a trade union.

It took Britain's first woman prime minister, Margaret Thatcher, to put a brake on union power. She pushed through a series of acts of parliament, against a background of violent strikes among mineworkers, newspaper workers and others, that broke the grip of the unions on the workplace and restored them to a more temperate role in workers' affairs.

TODAY

Striking fire-fighters on a picket line in Stirling, Scotland during a national strike in 2002–3, stand by a footpath brazier to keep warm.

1900

The morning church service over, the congregation in their Sunday best walk home to Sunday lunch down Brading High Street, Isle of Wight.

FLOURISHING CHRISTIANITY

Christianity has been the most important religion in the UK for fifteen centuries. It is the faith that the great majority of Britons – who may be Anglican, Catholic or nonconformist – put on passport and census forms, the latter for the first time in the 2001 census. There is a distinction to be made, however, between 'community size' and 'active membership' figures, and the number of people who actively follow a Christian life has been falling.

Christianity in Britain remains richly varied and diverse. People from many different cultures have migrated to Britain since the Middle Ages, bringing their kind of Christianity with them. Communities of Greek and Coptic Orthodox churches, Armenian, Lutheran and Reformed churches from all over Europe can be found in large cities such as London.

Out-numbering them are growing numbers of lively communities of charismatic and Pentecostal churches, boosted by immigration from the Caribbean since World War II.

TODAY

The choir in full voice at a packed session of the nonconformist Morris Cerullo Mission at Earl's Court in London.

*c.***1900**

The tin bath has been taken out into the back yard and these little ones are enjoying splashing about in the sunshine and getting clean as well.

BATHTIME

The tin hipbath, brought out on Saturday nights and set up in front of the kitchen range for all the family to use one after the other – starting with father – survived in many working-class households until after World War II, along with chamber pots and outside lavatories.

Rooms set aside solely for the bath and lavatory became the norm rather than the exception when new housing was built to replace bomb-damaged housing and slums. Now everyone except the very poor could enjoy the proper bathrooms – with hot and cold running water and inside lavatories – that the better-off had known for most of the century.

A modern bathroom is often a much more luxurious affair – not just a room in which to get clean, but somewhere to relax, perhaps surrounded by aromatherapy candles, and let the cares and anxieties of modern life be washed away. It is also the place to use the shampoos, deodorants, body mists, defoliating creams, depilatories and the many other treatments that have made the toiletries industry so profitable.

TODAY

Bathtime for the modern family is not just about getting clean. It is a time for fathers to bond with their children in 'quality time' play.

193

THE RAILWAY AGE

Railways were pioneered in Britain early in the nineteenth century. The 1830 opening of the Liverpool to Manchester Line, which carried both people and goods, triggered a massive railway boom during which, while fortunes were made and lost, a great railway network was built. By 1912 it covered over 18,000 miles (11,160 kilometres) and brought most people in Britain within reasonable reach of a train.

Despite a wide-ranging closure of unprofitable lines in the 1960s, Britain still has 20,000 miles (32,000 kilometres) of railway track and 2,500 railway stations, even though many small ones were sold off, their tracks lifted and the station buildings converted to houses and offices.

Today, the railways are fighting back against the competition of road and air transport. Inter-city services have been speeded up and local services have been transformed by the introduction of light railways in and between cities. So far, there are five light railways in operation in England and more planned. Britain's railway age still has a long run ahead.

TODAY
The light rail service, the Docklands Light Railway, connects London's Docklands with surrounding areas and the City of London.

EATING OUT

In between-the-wars Britain, most people ate
at home except on special occasions and only
the well-off – dressed formally in evening
jackets and evening gowns – regularly ate out
at smart hotels and restaurants, where they
were served by waiters in tails.

Eating out became much more relaxed and
informal once the 'consumer society' got into
its stride in the 1950s. Rising wages gave
people more money to spend and the package
holiday introducing millions to the foods of
other countries. Soon, such foods were
available in Britain, in French-style bistros,
Italian trattorias and pizza houses. Alongside
them, American-style burger bars were rapidly
outnumbering fish and chip shops as the
nation's main suppliers of 'fast food'.

Today, eating out in Britain can still mean
dining in formal style in a very expensive
restaurant run by a chef as celebrated as most
of his guests. It can also mean enjoying a slice
of pizza or a baguette with an exotic filling and
a cappuccino in a cardboard cup at a metal
table outside a coffee shop.

TODAY

The old idea that no respectable
person would be seen eating in the
street has long gone from Britain.
Fast-food outlets are too tempting.

1926

Two be-gowned undergraduates of Cambridge University discuss life from the saddles of their 'sit-up-and-beg' bicycles.

UNIVERSITIES

Educating good numbers of the country's young to a high standard became important when Britain became an industrialized society, which is why so many technical colleges and places offering practical advanced learning were founded in Britain during the course of the nineteenth century.

A university education remained something for a minority of young people until well after World War II, although the 1944 Education Act, which established secondary education for all, at least ensured plenty of potential students from among those who obtained good results in their final school year examinations.

University education began a great expansion in the 1960s, with the founding of new universities – including the Open University – and polytechnics and the conversion of many other higher-education foundations to full university status.

Today, the state, which puts much more funding into higher education than nineteenth-century governments would have thought necessary or desirable, would like to see half the country's young people undertaking some form of higher education.

TODAY

All that hard work at school has paid off for this girl, waving the A-level results that will get her into university at her overjoyed mother.

AT THE OFFICE

In Britain's offices, most workers, apart from a few typists, were male until World War I sent so many of them into the trenches that women had to step in and fill the gaps.

The office environment would have seemed austere to present-day workers. It involved much hand-written paperwork and office administration was a disciplined paternalism. There was no smoking, and meals, often supplied by managements, were conducted in a military fashion, with departmental breaks taken at contracted eating places. Grey suits were the rule, although sports jackets were permitted on Saturday mornings.

The average modern office is well lit and air-conditioned and its staff is a mixed-sex one. Dress is informal – even City of London offices have dress-down Fridays – and, as eighty years ago, smoking is forbidden. As well as the obvious differences made by electronics and computer technology, the modern office differs from that of eighty years ago by offering fewer opportunities for getting together: the office e-mail system is no substitute for talk.

TODAY

Shirt-sleeved staff put together another edition of the *Daily Mirror* newspaper in the newsroom of the paper's London office.

201

OBSERVING THE SABBATH

The small Jewish community in England, well established by the eighteenth century and with its own synagogue in Aldgate, London, was greatly enlarged from the 1880s onward by Jews fleeing persecution in Europe and Russia.

The largest communities of Jews in Britain were to be found in the East End of London, particularly in Whitechapel, where their particular trade was tailoring. Jews were largely responsible for establishing the ready-made suits and clothing trade in Britain.

The Jewish community in Britain remains relatively small, coming fifth on the religion membership table, after Christians, Muslims, Hindus and Sikhs. Like other religions, Jews fall into separate groupings, orthodox Jews being the most strict in their observance of religious laws. After many years' discussion, orthodox Jews succeeded in 2003 in having an *eruv* marked out in Golders Green, London, within which they may relax their observance of some of the very strict laws governing their behaviour on the Sabbath.

TODAY

An orthodox Jewish father and his child admire the poles and fine wire that mark out the 11-mile (18-km) *eruv* set up in London in 2003.

203

MOTORWAYS

Britain became a car-owning society after World War II, when the number of cars on the roads doubled from pre-war numbers within ten years of the war and doubled again by the mid-1960s. At the same time, road haulage, which had grown rapidly before the war, also surged ahead. All this traffic had to go somewhere and in the 1950s Britain began building motorways, following the example of Italy and Germany, which had built their first motorways before the war.

The first stretch of real motorway, as distinct from improved trunk roads, was the Preston bypass in Lancashire, opened in 1958. Within a year, the 'Great White Way' from London to Birmingham, now part of the M1, was opened.

Today, there are 2,126 miles (3,422 kilometres) of motorways in Britain. They may account for less than one per cent of the country's total road network, but they carry 20 per cent of the traffic. And they are always busy – too busy, holidaymakers trapped in bank holiday jams would say. Unlike Europe's motorways, Britain's are free, but perhaps for not much longer.

1935
The No. 1 platform at Paddington
Station in the GWR's centenary year
is not much changed from the
platform that Brunel built.

PADDINGTON & THE GWR

'God's Wonderful Railway' was how its
employees once described the Great Western
Railway. They probably meant not the deity but
the builder of the line from London to Bristol –
the great railway engineer, bridge builder and
ship builder, Isambard Kingdom Brunel.

Brunel was appointed engineer of the Great
Western Railway in 1833 and between 1835
and 1841 built the GWR and all its tunnels,
bridges and viaducts. He designed its stations,
too, the most splendid of which was the
London terminal, Paddington Station.

Today, spruced up and refurbished,
Paddington Station is a thoroughly modern
railway terminus linked to Heathrow Airport by
a fast electric train service and providing
hundreds of services a day to the west of
England and south Wales. It has returned, in
part, to the great days of the Railway Age, for
there are private rail companies at Paddington
again, including Great Western.

TODAY
A multi-million-pound refurbishment
in the late 1990s revealed the glory
of Brunel's great glass-and-iron roof
at Paddington Station.

CHANGING INDUSTRY

The dark satanic mills that William Blake wrote about were, in his day, black spots on an otherwise green and pleasant land. But mills and factories meant wealth and, helped by the growth of steam power and the railway, spread over large parts of Britain, which became the workshop of the world.

In Yorkshire, where there were nearly 900 mills by 1850, Sheffield made steel in great sheets for industry and in fine sheets for cutlery. For generations of Britons in all parts of the Empire, the only acceptable tableware was cutlery from Sheffield.

Smoke-belching chimneys no longer dominate Sheffield's skyline. Some mills have been preserved as magnificent examples of industrial history and others have been converted to high-quality housing. And the city's engineering heritage is in the care of Sheffield University's Faculty of Engineering, one of the best in the country.

TODAY

A knife-maker at work in Sheffield, where cutlery is still made to a high standard but in much smaller quantities than in earlier times.

Miners bringing up trucks of coal at
the Cresswell Colliery, near Mansfield
in Nottinghamshire, where coal
mines were prosperous and modern.

FROM COAL TO OIL & GAS

From the reign of Elizabeth I to the reign of
Elizabeth II, coal was a primary source of heat
and power in Britain's homes, offices and
factories. Today, it is not. It has been overtaken
by other fossil fuels, oil and natural gas, much
of which comes from the North Sea.

The North Sea oil and gas industries got
into gear in the 1970s, at much the same time
that coal mines were becoming unproductive
and expensive to operate. A series of bitter
strikes in the 1980s sounded the death knell of
an industry that had been part of the nation's
culture for centuries.

Today, the UK is the world's tenth largest
producer of crude oil and gas, and nearly
three-quarters of the country's energy
consumption is in the form of oil and natural
gas. We still use a lot of coal, to make
electricity and to have friendly open fires at
home and in the pub, but it no longer provides
work and a way of life for whole communities.

TODAY

On the drilling deck of the
Ben Reoch oil rig in the East Brae
field in the North Sea.

211

1908

A botany class in progress at a girls' school in London. The smock-clad girls are sitting at desks that would still be in use fifty years later.

EDUCATION

Primary education for all children became compulsory in Britain in the 1870s. Every town and village in the land had a school, many of them run by the different churches, where children were taught to read, write, and do sums. For many years, boys and girls were separated, both in class and in the playground. They sat in bench-like desks set in neat lines, facing their teacher and the blackboard.

In the days before radio, television and other distractions, many children filled their time out of school with occupations complementary to their school work. Children might collect and press the flowers they studied in botany, or put plant and flower cards, taken from their father's cigarette packs, into albums.

Primary school teaching has become child-centred in mixed classes. Children are encouraged to be individuals, while working in groups. But some things do not change. The school playground is still a place where children can leap about and let off steam and many of the games they play were played by their grandparents at the turn of the century.

TODAY
Children playing hopscotch in the playground of a mixed primary school in Glasgow, Scotland.

QUEUING: A VERY BRITISH HABIT

Forming orderly queues to obtain anything from stamps in the post office and tickets at the cinema to a seat on the bus has long been a sensible British habit.

During World War II it became almost a way of life as shoppers queued in all weathers, ration books at the ready, to buy permitted quantities of many basic foods. Rationing, first imposed in 1940, did not end until 1953.

Queuing used to be a fine art, involving careful decisions about which queue to join. Except in the supermarket, that's no longer necessary. Now, one queue usually snakes back and forth across the available space, people peeling off when a ticket window or counter is free. The high point of the queuing year comes with the January sales. Shoppers – Christmas dinner hardly digested – take folding stools and sleeping bags for an overnight wait, to queue to be first through the doors on the opening day of their favourite store's sale.

TODAY

Queuing, sometimes overnight, to be first in the door at the January sales is a fine British custom. Here, Glasgow shoppers are lining up.

1946

A general view of 'Britain's £20,000 civilian aerodrome at Heath Row', nearing completion and intended to be the country's main air junction.

GETTING ABOUT BY AIR

When Britain's biggest 'aerodrome' fully opened near the small Middlesex village of Heath Row in 1948, tents and Nissen huts left over from the War housed administration offices and passenger facilities.

The extraordinarily rapid growth in air travel within the UK and to destinations all round the world meant not only that Heathrow had to be enlarged again and again but also that many other airports had to be built – and enlarged – in all parts of the country.

Today, there are more then 150 licensed civil aerodromes in the UK, handling between them at the latest count over 181 million passengers a year and 2.3 million tonnes of freight. Heathrow is the world's busiest airport for international travellers, and Gatwick is the world's sixth busiest. The tents and Nissen huts have long gone, of course, and today's big airports have shopping malls, cafés and multi-ethnic restaurants to ease the wait for flights.

TODAY

Moving walkways like this one at Manchester Airport help passengers make the long walk between terminal and departure gate.

217

1936
Sixty-eight-year-old Mr T W Hills, at work in the GPO's Barking Depot, was London's oldest and only bearded postman.

CITY DELIVERIES

Nothing beats the man and woman on foot or bicycle for delivering goods to the door in towns and cities. They don't have to worry about finding somewhere to park a vehicle; nor do they get stuck in traffic jams.

The Post Office, founded in 1635, has provided a town postal delivery service on foot since Victorian times and the post is still the most essential, walk-based delivery service in towns and cities today. The postie may have a bike, rather than a smart trolley, with a large leather bag on front, but for most of the daily route, the bike is pushed rather than ridden.

There has been a great burgeoning of private sector couriers and express delivery mail services in Britain since the Post Office lost its monopoly, though private mail-delivery operators must charge a minimum fee for each delivery they undertake. Beating city traffic has been the major reason for the big increase in non-mail cycle courier services in towns and cities. The courier on a bike or motorcycle can get the pizza or takeaway to the front door while it is still hot from the oven.

TODAY
Couriers, often wearing masks to ward off traffic fumes, quickly deliver anything small from letters to pizzas in towns and cities.

1936
A Cornish housewife checks how a tray of pasties are getting on in her beautifully black-leaded coal-fired kitchen range.

KITCHENS

A heavy closed range, made of cast-iron and fired by wood or coal, became the main feature of kitchens during the Victorian era. Food was cooked in it, water was heated on it, and clothes were dried round it. It also kept the kitchen – and the whole house, if small – warm and snug.

The harnessing of gas and electricity as a cooking fuel changed everything. Closed ranges, which had once seemed the ultimate in convenience compared with open fires, were now torn out of kitchens in town and country. They were replaced by gas and electric cookers or, especially in country kitchens, by efficient new ranges, fired by gas, oil or electricity and with electric thermostats.

The modern kitchen is seldom the heart of the household, that role having been taken by the living room and the television. For many, the kitchen is either the place for quickly heating ready-prepared meals or a sort of space-age laboratory where the many highways and by-ways of gastronomy can be explored by people able to buy the ingredients of all the world's cuisines at the supermarket.

TODAY
This very stylish modern kitchen, essential utensils and cookbooks ready to hand, has its gas cooking hob separate from the oven.

1956
The first Hindu wedding to take place at India House, the office of the India High Commission in London, nears completion.

HINDUS IN BRITAIN

Most of the members of the Hindu community in Britain today originate from India, once the 'jewel in the crown' of the British Empire, though other Hindus have come from other former colonial territories, mostly in Africa, to which Indians migrated.

The first Indians to reach Britain came as servants of merchants returning home, having made their fortune in India. They were few in number and Indians, both Hindu and Muslim, were not seen in large numbers in Britain until they were encouraged to come to relieve the intense labour shortage after World War II.

Hindu communities are close-knit and their culture is important to them. London's Hindus demonstrated their devotion to Hindu culture and religion in the 1990s by raising within the community the money to build the magnificent Shri Swaminarayan Temple in London, the first purpose-built Hindu temple in Europe. Much of the marble for the temple was prepared and carved in India by master craftsmen and then transported to Britain.

TODAY
The building of the Shri Swaminarayan Hindu Temple in Neasden, North London, was paid for by the Hindu community.

1940

An unexploded bomb is no reason for not delivering the milk. To save precious fuel, the milkman uses horsepower to pull his milk float.

DELIVERING THE GOODS

The Victorians, with their railway lines reaching into all parts of the country, moved into the business of home deliveries with enthusiasm.

The post, milk, bread and newspapers were at the everyday end of a system that in time included huge mail order catalogues from businesses such as the Army & Navy Stores, which offered to deliver everything from corsets to cricket pavilions to the ends of the Empire.

Even when war came to the Home Front in 1940, deliveries of essential goods still got through – both in town and country – however hazardous unexploded bombs made the job.

The home delivery business flourishes in Britain, given new impetus by the internet. People can sit at home and tick off on a screen the items on the weekly shopping list, sit back and wait to have them delivered to the front door, where the milkman, paper boy, postman and perhaps the local pizza restaurant will have already delivered their goods.

TODAY

A child helps her mother unload a delivery ordered by telephone, e-mail or via the Internet, from a local supermarket.

225

CELEBRATIONS **7**

1953
Cardboard periscopes at the ready, huge crowds fill Trafalgar Square, ready to cheer Elizabeth II after her coronation on June 2.

ROYAL JUBILEE

Half a century ago, on June 2, 1953, the coronation of Elizabeth II brought crowds flocking into London from all over the country and the Commonwealth, eager for a glimpse of the young woman whose father's death a year before had made her queen. Many people had waited for days for the big event, and pouring rain did not dampen their enthusiasm.

Fifty years after that unexpected accession, London's streets were once again hung with banners and flags and were full of enthusiastic crowds, eager to celebrate with the Queen her fifty years on the throne.

The Queen and Prince Philip drove to the service in St Paul's Cathedral in the same ornate gold coach that had taken her to her coronation. They came back up the crowd-filled Mall to watch an afternoon of parades and fun from the steps of the Victoria Memorial, then went to the balcony of Buckingham Palace to watch a unique 27-aircraft flypast. The atmosphere and excitement of the day showed that patriotism has not disappeared in an age of scepticism and doubt.

TODAY
Union flags flutter as the large crowd in The Mall watch the flypast that was part of the Golden Jubilee celebrations in 2002.

1956
The first stopping place for these new arrivals in England from the West Indies is the Customs Hall at Southampton docks.

NOTTING HILL CARNIVAL

Although many Britons grew rich on the West Indian sugar trade in the great days of Empire, few Caribbeans came to Britain.

Things changed after World War II, when a severe labour shortage in Britain led the government to promote the idea of finding work in Britain to people in the West Indies, where there was high unemployment. The first boatload of Jamaicans reached Britain in 1948. They were followed by thousands more and the UK's West Indian communities grew rapidly.

The Notting Hill Carnival began as a small, impromptu event among West Indians living in London's Notting Hill, notorious in the 1950s for its serious racial tensions. In 1965 a few of them brought their steel bands out into the street and began playing. Today, the Notting Hill Carnival is a colourful extravaganza of music, dancing and fantastic costume that brings hundreds of thousands of people of all races to Notting Hill to take part in the fun.

TODAY
The Notting Hill Carnival, an exuberant display of Caribbean culture, is the largest street carnival in Europe.

It is Burns' Night, the haggis has been piped in and is about to be stabbed, doused in whisky and served with champit tatties and bashed neeps.

SCOTLAND CELEBRATES

The two greatest nights of celebration in Scotland's year come within weeks of each other in the depths of winter, when the glowing warmth provided by whisky, the Scots' national spirit, is very welcome.

Hogmanay, or New Year's Eve, is celebrated by many Scots at home, with visitors offered black bun and copious amounts of whisky. The ideal first visitor, or First Foot, of Hogmanay is dark-haired or carries a lump of coal to signify the wish that the home fire will burn brightly throughout the coming year. In Scotland's big cities, Hogmanay is an excuse for revelry all night among the crowds filling city streets.

On January 25, Scots and non-Scots all over the world celebrate the birth of Robert Burns, the country's greatest poet. As well as reciting Robert Burns' poetry, the ceremony of Burns' Night is centred on the haggis, a surprisingly tasty mixture of offal and oats, served with potatoes, swede and plenty of whisky.

TODAY
There is no difficulty in guessing which Hogmanay these young people are celebrating with a swim in the Firth of Forth.

Driving off in a horse-drawn carriage after their marriage will give this newly wed couple another happy memory of their wedding day.

MARRIAGE, BRITISH-STYLE

Marriage demonstrates more startlingly than anything else the great cultural and social changes that have come over Britain in the past two or three generations.

As recently as the mid-1970s, few people lived openly together without being married and the majority of marriage ceremonies took place in a religious building.

Three things changed this situation: a rapidly rising divorce rate, a dramatic fall in the number of people for whom church-going was an important part of life, and the fact that many people no longer saw any stigma attached to having children outside marriage.

The majority of men and women in Britain still think marriage is an ideal state. Recent legislation has given them a wide choice of venues other than churches to get married in. Places from castles to coal mines, football clubs to country inns, can apply for a licence to hold civil marriage services.

TODAY

It was Red Nose Day when this couple got married in chapel at Lurgan, Co Armagh, so they decided to raise money for Comic Relief.

1939

Everyone is in their best clothes and on their best behaviour at this birthday party, which is taking place in the birthday-girl's back garden.

BIRTHDAYS

Whatever gloomy pundits may say, family bonds remain strong, and in few areas of family life is this more so than when it comes to children's birthday parties: every child, including one-year-olds, must have one.

Before World War II, birthday parties were usually organized at home. Children came in their best clothes – party frocks for girls and white shirts and ties for even relatively small boys – and played organized games before sitting down at an orderly tea-table with the birthday cake in the centre.

Things are different today, when children tend to have greater expectations. Although birthdays remain traditional in essentials – games, lots of food and a cake – parties tend to take place away from home and parents spend a lot more on them. Entertainers such as clowns may come to the house to delight smaller children, but older children expect to be taken out, perhaps to the cinema, where they are given the run of the pick'n'mix stall in the foyer, with a pizza or Big Mac to follow. It's great for kids, exhausting for parents.

TODAY

Throwing themselves into the spirit of the occasion on a bouncy castle, these children are enjoying a birthday party away from home.

REMEMBRANCE SUNDAY

The guns of World War I fell silent at 11am on November 11, 1918. Ever since, November 11 has been Armistice Day in Britain. For a week or so before, many people wear poppies in memory of the men who lost their lives in the poppy fields of Flanders and for those from the British Empire and Commonwealth who lost their lives in the many conflicts, large and small, that followed the Great War.

The anniversary of Armistice Day is marked in London by a wreath-laying service in Whitehall, around the Cenotaph designed by the architect Edwin Lutyens, which was unveiled on Armistice Day in 1920.

Some years ago, to avoid bringing London to a standstill on a weekday, the wreath-laying ceremony was moved to the Sunday nearest November 11. Every year, on a Sunday morning in November, central London falls silent as the Queen leads the nation in remembering the men and women who died for their countries.

TODAY

The Queen has seldom missed leading the nation in homage to its war dead, and she is the first to lay a wreath on the Cenotaph's steps.

CHINESE NEW YEAR

It is the tradition in China to visit relatives and distribute presents, symbols of goodwill and good fortune at the start of the new year, which is given a new animal name. These New Year traditions are celebrated in great style by Britain's Chinese population.

Communities of Chinese people developed in several of Britain's big cities in the twentieth century. Some set up restaurants or shops selling oriental foods and other goods that were becoming fashionable in Britain. Others came to work in the sweatshops of the clothing industry in the East End of London.

Chinese New Year is now celebrated every year, especially in London, in a style that is enjoyed as much by British people and foreign visitors as by the Chinese themselves. London's Chinatown holds a huge and colourful parade, featuring beautiful models of dragons and performances of the lion dance, to enliven the wintry streets of Soho every January.

THE LORD MAYOR'S SHOW

You wouldn't think it, looking at the scantily clad girls, the dancers and the exotic animals, but the fact is that there is a solemn reason for the Lord Mayor's Show, which brings traffic chaos to the City of London every second Saturday in November.

In 1215, King John granted a charter to the City of London that gave it the right to elect a Mayor every year. A condition was that the mayor should present himself to his sovereign, or to a representative, to swear 'fealty' and to be approved. This is what the City of London's new Lord Mayor is doing when he drives in procession to the Law Courts every year.

The Lord Mayor was first accompanied by a procession on his way to swear loyalty to the crown in the sixteenth century and he still travels – very uncomfortably – in a magnificent coach built in 1757. It is only proper that his coach should be grand, for in the City he ranks above everyone else except the Queen.

TODAY
The Lord Mayor's Show has become an excuse for a carnival in the City of London, typified by this colourful float and dancers.

GREAT LIFE EXPECTATIONS

In the early years of her reign, it was not an
arduous task for Elizabeth II to send the by
now traditional congratulatory telegram to
those of her subjects in Britain and the
Commonwealth who reached the notable age
of 100. There were not too many of them.
Today, there are a great many more, including,
in 2000, the Queen's own mother.

Life expectancy rose greatly for men and
women in the twentieth century. In 1901, the
life expectancy of a man was 48 years; by 1998
it had risen to nearly 75 years. For women, the
figures have risen from 51.6 years to almost 80.

Britons are living longer for many reasons.
Rising standards of living, healthier eating
habits, and enormous advances in medicine
and medical technology have helped adults live
much longer. Perhaps 100 will come to seem
so commonplace a birthday that Elizabeth II's
successors will stop sending congratulatory
telegrams to those subjects who reach it.

1961

The infants of Queen's Park Primary School in Harlesden, London, concentrate hard on their roles in the school's nativity play.

CHRISTMAS

The Victorians added the Christmas card, the Christmas tree and the idea of giving everyone (rather than just the servants on Boxing Day) presents to the way we celebrate the birth of Christ. All too soon, it was no longer enough for the village choir to rehearse a special Christmas anthem for everyone to listen to in church and then go home to a more special dinner than usual.

While the real meaning of Christmas has become submerged in modern Britain's consumer culture, it is by no means lost. Christmas remains for most people a time for making a special effort to bring families together. Churches are much fuller at Christmas for a range of special services than at any other time of the year except Easter.

For many children, their first introduction to the magic and mystery of the Christmas message comes at school. The infant class's annual performance of the nativity play, in which as many children as possible get a part, remains for many of the children and their parents a lifelong memory.

TODAY

Ronald Briggs' 'Snowman' is the theme of this specially decorated shop window, designed to get people into a festive, buying mood.

1923

Admiring one of the wells
decorated for Ascension Day
during the well dressing at Tissington
in Derbyshire.

WELL DRESSING

Wells – being sources of water, the most essential thing in life – were venerated and even worshipped in many pagan religions, including the Romans'. In Britain, the custom of dressing the village well is an ancient one and is still carried on in many places. The Derbyshire Peak District is the main centre of well dressing, with dozens of towns and villages having well-dressing ceremonies every year.

Although well dressings are usually closely tied to the church calendar, and take place between May and September every year, some villages link their ceremonies to other events, such as the village carnival or a bank holiday.

The village of Tissington, near Ashbourne in Derbyshire, holds its well-dressing ceremonies on Ascension Day every year and the village's five wells are all dressed. This is not just a matter of draping some greenery over the well. Dressing the wells at Tissington involves the making of elaborate picture boards, with the pictures made of petals, flowers, leaves and other natural objects pressed into a layer of clay. They are very impressive.

TODAY

Hands Well is built in a commanding position at the top of the village of Tissington. The well's decoration is re-designed every year.

EASTER

Easter, the time of Christ's crucifixion and resurrection, is the most important part of the Christian year. Many of the traditions and customs associated with Easter date back centuries and some are associated with pre-Christian rituals and beliefs.

Although Easter has lost its religious importance for many people, it still retains a greater religious significance than Christmas, and the customs and traditions of the period – from distributing greenery on Palm Sunday and the giving of Maundy Money by the Queen on Maundy Thursday, to eating hot-cross buns on Good Friday – remain very popular.

The giving of eggs, symbols of birth, resurrection and new life, is the predominant Easter custom. Children, in particular, learn something of the meaning of Easter in Easter Sunday festivals in churches or when hunting for Easter eggs among the spring flowers in their garden. Egg-rolling is another Easter tradition that children take part in with gusto. At Avenham Park in Preston hundreds of youngsters take part in the annual Easter egg-rolling.

TODAY
These children have done well in their hunt for Easter eggs, hidden among the flowers in their garden in Keith, Aberdeenshire.

251

EISTEDDFODAU IN WALES

The special festivals called eisteddfodau have long held a special place in Welsh cultural life. They celebrate and encourage literature and music, both of which have very long traditions in Wales. Welsh literature, which many believe can be traced back to the Druids, is one of the oldest literatures in Europe.

The first recorded eisteddfod in Wales was in 1176. It was not until the early nineteenth century that the tradition of crowning the best bard of the year began. From this time, too, many rituals purporting to date back to the times of the Druids began to be introduced into the ceremonial of the eisteddfod.

Two particularly important eisteddfodau are held in Wales every year. The Royal National Eisteddfod, held in a different town each year, has competitions in music, singing, prose and poetry in Welsh. The International Music Eisteddfod, held in Llangollen, attracts performers from all over the world.

INDEX

PICTURE CREDITS

The publishers would like to thank the following sources for their kind permission to reproduce the pictures in this book:

AKG London: 6, 98, 118.

Alamy Images: /Peter Bowater: **245**; /Elvele Images: **83**; /Robert Harding Picture Library: **23**.

Janice Anderson & Edmund Swinglehurst: 1, 20.

Billie Love Historical Collection: 50, 70, 148, 184, 190, 236.

The Birmingham Alliance: /Bullring Birmingham opens September 2003. Picture courtesy of the developer, The Birmingham Alliance: **175**.

Bubbles Photo Library: /Nikki Gibbs: **237**; /Angela Hampton: **25**; /Loisjoy Thurstun: **251**.

Collections: /Phil Crean: **125**; /Robert Estall: **33, 149**; /Nigel Hawkins: **75**; /Mike Kipling: **51**; /Select: **209**; /Liz Stares: **217**.

Corbis: /Adrian Arbib: **201**; /Richard Cummins: **155**; /E. O. Hoppé: **160, 178, 240**; /Hulton-Deutsch Collection: **222, 230, 242, 244, 248**; /Richard Klune: **27**; /Rob Matheson: **179**; /Chris North/Cordaiy Photo Library: **163**; /PicImpact: **85**; /Michael St. Maur Sheil: **47**; /Alan Towse/Ecoscene: **136**; /Underwood & Underwood: **46**; /Patrick Ward: **31**.

EMPICS: /Mike Egerton: **97**.

Ffotograff: /Charles Aithie: **167**.

The Francis Frith Collection: 158.

© **FreeFoto.com:** /Ian Britton: **169**.

Getty Images: /S. & N. Geary: **161**; /Julian Herbert: **111**; /Bay Hippisley: **221**; /Hulton Archive: **12, 18, 22, 26, 32, 34, 38, 58, 62, 78, 84, 108, 120, 138, 150, 154, 156, 164, 166, 168, 170, 172, 174, 176, 180, 186, 194, 208**; /Clive Mason: **103, 105**; /Stephen Munday: **119**; /Timothy Shonnard: **193**; /Paul Thomas: **219**; /Mark Thompson: **89**; /Sion Touhig: **101**.

Glasgow City Council: /DRS Graphics/Stephen Hosey: **181**.

S. & R. Greenhill: /Sally Greenhill: **45**.

Marc Henrie: 79.

Lancashire Evening Post: /Iain Lynn: **159**.

Ken Lees: 117.

Mary Evans Picture Library: 44, 112; /Barry Norman: **124**.

National Trust Photographic Library: /Stephen Robson: **65**.
Ocado: /Ocado in partnership with Waitrose. Photographer: Mike O'Dwyer: **225**.

PA Photos: /Paul Faith: **235**; /Yui Mok: **21**; /Stefan Rousseau: **239**; /Michael Stephens: **243**.

Pictures of Britain: /Dorothy Burrows: **249**; /Deryck L. Hallam: **173**; /Bernard Humphries: **151**; /Julian Worker: **59**.

Redferns: /Simon King: **35**.

Rex Features: /Nigel R. Barklie: **171, 207**; /David Bebber: **19**; /Adrian Brooks: **195**; /Denis Cameron: **247**; /Mark Campbell: **13**; /Clive Dixon: **15, 41**; /Andrew Drysdale: **187**; /James Fraser: **233**; /Richard Gardner: **139**; /Brian Harris: **205**; /Nils Jorgensen: **29**; /Robert Judges: **199**; /Tom Kidd: **129**; /Charles Knight: **39**; /Herbie Knott: **121**; /Tony Kyriacou: **241**; /Richard Mildenhall: **143**; /Andrew Milligan: **189**; /Jeroen Oerlemans: **231**; /Peter Price: **185**; /Brian Rasic: **107**; /Tim Rooke: **93**; /SIPA Press: **223**; /South West News: **141**; /South West News/Chris Ison: **131**; /Jeremy Sutton Hibbert: **213**; /Ray Tang: **57, 67**; /Andrew Terrill: **137**; /TimePix/Margaret Bourke-White: **66**; /Times Newspapers Ltd: **191**; /R. G. Williamson: **157**.

Royal Botanic Gardens, Kew: 40.

Scottish Viewpoint: /Wattie Cheung: **215**; /Drew Farrell: **91**; /Colin McPherson: **77**; /Tina Norris: **49**; /Paul Tomkins/VisitScotland: **43, 63, 99**.

Penny Simpson: 200.

Nigel Sutton: 203.

Topham: 2, 8tr, 8br, 8bl, 14, 16, 24, 28, 30, 42, 48, 54, 55, 56, 60, 68, 80, 88, 90, 92, 96, 100, 104, 110, 114, 116, 122, 128, 130, 134, 142, 144, 145, 146, 162, 188, 192, 196, 197, 198, 202, 204, 206, 210, 211, 212, 214, 216, 218, 220, 224, 228, 232, 234, 238, 246, 250, 252; /Stewart Galloway: 10-11, 52-53, 86-87, 126-127, 152-153, 182-183, 226-227; /HIP: 82, 94, 132; /HIP/Museum of London: 76; /HIP/National Motor Museum: 8tl, 36, 74, 102; /PA Photos: 64, 69, 73, 81, 95, 109, 115, 123, 135, 147, 177, 229, 253; /PAL/Clive Barda: 113; /Ponopresse: 140; /PressNet: 17, 106; /Ray Roberts: 133; /UPPA: 37, 61, 71, 72, 165.

Every effort has been made to acknowledge correctly and contact the source and/or copyright holder of each picture and Carlton Books Limited apologises for any unintentional errors or omissions which will be corrected in future editions of this book.

FOREWORD BY PETER SISSONS

What is it about Britain that makes the images in this book so evocative, and so important historically?

'Typically British' is one of the most over-used phrases, and not just in the English language. For me, what lies at the heart of this phrase, is our greatest national treasure – the freedom of expression. In Britain this freedom is the mother of every other national characteristic – especially inventiveness, ingenuity, and tolerance.

The British are adaptable and adventurous. They are excited by things that are new, but they don't trust them until they are tried and tested. The story of Britain is the story of steady change.

For well over a hundred years now, since reliable photography became commonplace, we've been able to record that change – and the pictures are fascinating across the whole of British life.

The British are a sporting nation, and the great fixtures of the sporting year, Wimbledon, Cup Final, Lords, Twickenham and Boat Race are national institutions – but they've changed. The British enjoy their leisure, and have always believed they're entitled to it, whatever hand life has dealt them – but they'll change their habits, if it's change for the better.

They enjoy their entertainment too. In the late fifties, a new generation – not yet slaves to TV and the Internet – made their own entertainment, and British popular music caught the imagination of young and old across the world.

The British still value the concept of fair play. Their political parties vie with each other in promising social improvement and the alleviation of hardship. It's a national pastime to complain about how slowly social conditions change, but change they do. The centres of most of our great cities bear eloquent witness.

A Briton's home is their castle, and improvements to both the home and garden – if you believe the TV schedulers – border on a national obsession.

The British are also a fighting nation. Two world wars, and many lesser conflicts, have left their scars and their badges of pride.

The Britain of yesterday was different, but it made Britain what it is today. Inside these pages you'll see what I mean…

INTRODUCTION

The United Kingdom of Great Britain and Northern Ireland has much to be proud of and much to celebrate. We pack into a comparatively small space some of the world's most beautiful countryside, where rolling green and gold farmland and 'blue remembered hills' are studded with lakes, lochs and tarns and watered by great rivers and sparkling streams. Our towns and cities include some that are among the most architecturally handsome and innovative in the world. Our society is essentially peaceful and well ordered, set on a firmly democratic base in which we all have a say, through the ballot box, in what goes on nationally and at a local level.

Things are not like this for many other countries in the world, and they were not always like this for us. Britain yesterday – in the nineteenth and early twentieth centuries – was an imperial power and a nation that relied on its industries, most of them in the Midlands and the north of England, for most of its great wealth and for the income of the bulk of its people. Today, sociologists and historians tell us, we are a post-industrial society, whose once-mighty industrial base has dwindled to a shadow of its former might and in which an entirely different kind of economy, based on 'invisible earnings' and service industries, directs the way in which we live our lives and choose the ways by which we earn our living.

During the move from an industrial world to a post-industrial one, our standards of living improved dramatically, though not without many difficulties. Today, the welfare of the individual is an essential concern, education is a universal right, adult men and women all have the vote, and many kinds of leisure can be enjoyed by everyone in the free time that shorter working hours and longer paid holidays have given us.

All this has happened during a time when science and technology have progressed at breathtaking speed. On the way, they have given us steam propulsion of many kinds – including railways and ships – the telegraph, electric light, sewage systems, paved roads, the internal combustion engine, powered flight, radio communications and many, many more benefits, most of which were little more than a gleam in scientists' eyes when Prince Albert opened the Great Exhibition in London's Hyde Park in 1851.

Today, Britain is again one of the world's most prosperous nations. It is a country where the bulk of the population, who once rarely saw foreign faces, now lives in a multi-ethnic society where many races and religions live together in remarkable peace and harmony. It is a country whose people, who once ate mostly roast beef or boiled mutton, are now connoisseurs of pasta, pizza, Peking duck, Vindaloo curry, sushi and chili con carne. And it is a country where people still happily celebrate centuries-old traditions and customs in the midst of twenty-first-century technological wizardry.

This book is a celebration of all these aspects of life in Britain today, and of the adaptability, ingenuity and tolerance of the British people.